BIG BULLIES

Dan Louisell

Based on <u>Bullied,</u> a screenplay
by Dan Louisell and Angella Szynkowski
which was based on a story
by Dan Louisell

FROM THE AUTHOR

I have a lot of wonderful support from a lot of wonderful people for a lot of creative things I've done. Not all of them will like this book, and that is okay. It is admittedly not for everybody. It is distasteful, disrespectful, violent, and straight blasphemous if you're into that kind of thing. I think that kind of thing is very funny.

If you, reader, do not think those kinds of things are very funny, then you have my full permission to skip this book. If you choose to read the book anyway, you do not have my permission to be mad at me about something in this book you didn't like; including but not limited to grammar, syntax, spelling erorrs, lazy storytelling or inconsistent formatting.

I want to thank my friend Angella Szynkowski, who originally helped me turn this story into a completed screenplay from which this book is adapted. I also want to thank my wife Liz for encouraging me to finish the book by reading it in-progress and demanding an ending, and then proof-reading it, after which she complained about the ending.

For Your Mom.

PROLOGUE: Then and Now

He managed to shut his eyes just in time. *Splat!* Right in his ear. Wet cold slopped down the side of his face; his cheek stinging with the icy... sting. With his other ear he heard another splat from a few feet away followed by a string of swear words. In fact, they were these words: goddamn, fucking, shit, fuck, ass, fuck again, and cock.

"*Mother goddamn piece of fucking shit fuck ass! Fuck my cock!*"

That was the unmistakable eloquence of Eugene Campbell. Wes deducted that Eugene must have also been a victim of this malicious snowball attack. Wes's name wasn't Wes. Wes's name was Michael. But his last name was Westin. At some point when he was very young, everyone started calling

5

him *Wes*. Michael didn't care. And by *everyone*, it was mostly just Eugene who mostly was the only one who ever talked to Wes.

"I'm going to fucking feed your god damn ass to your balls, Evan!" Eugene shouted, being not quite old enough to really grasp the concept of cursing. "Down your cunt throat!" he added because he'd forgotten to say *cunt* up until then.

Wes and Eugene were both nine-years-old and just trying to mind their own business at recess. Evan, an eleven-year-old fifth grader must have taken offense to this because he decided they weren't covered in snowballs enough. Now they were both clumsily wiping melting snow clumps off their rosy cheeks and all was right in Even's world. He was a dick, you see, particularly to Wes and Eugene.

"I threw snow at you because you're fat, Wes."

"I figured you probably had a good reason," Wes told him, coolly. He was after all, slightly above average weight. Maybe that's why he and Eugene became friends in the first place. Eugene was short and skinny, and it just seemed like a good fit that the fat kind and the runt form an alliance.

"What's the matter, Wes? You gonna cry?" Evan was a dick, remember. "That's what your mom did when you were born!"

"Lots of people's moms cried because childbirth is painful *and you know that, Evan!*"

6

Wes tried initially to not raise his voice before realizing he had no reason not to shout. Who was he going to impress? What did it matter if he stayed cool or not?

"Well your mom cried extra because of all the extra pounds of stupid that came out with you! Out of her vagina hole!"

"Yeah," agreed Evan's sidekick Wade, who hadn't thrown any snowballs but was usually around to support Evan's dickery. "And after the doctor slapped you, he slapped your mom across the face, too. Just for being a bitch!" Good one, Wade.

"And then," Evan excitedly continued, "and then the doctor stabbed your dad!"

"My dad was stabbed outside of a Burlington Coat Factory *and you know that Evan!*" The stabbing of Wes's dad was on the news, after all.

"Yeah he was," Evan corrected himself. "Just for being a bitch!"

By this time a whole group of elementary school kids had gathered to see what was going on and all burst out laughing at the hilarious burn-ball Evan just dunked. Eugene started swearing again. Not with any real point, but more like a list of dirty words he knew. Wes was clutching a lunchbox in his right hand that Evan immediately snatched away. As Wes watched Evan raise the lunchbox up in the air out of his reach, he stared at the picture of the California Raisins looking back and smiling at him. How on Earth could they still be happy and singing in Evan's filthy bitch hands? Wes was irritated but not surprised, as this happened pretty often.

"Let's see what butts eat for lunch!" Evan said as he fumbled the lunchbox around looking for the latch.

"Leave that lunch alone, or I'll--" Eugene didn't get to finish his sentence, as his mouth was suddenly stopped by Wes's lunch box bashing against it, with Evan still holding the handle. It hit Eugene's face so hard, he toppled to the ground, landing in his back.

"Fuck my cock!" he managed to say.

Evan beckoned Wade to his side. He opened the lunch box and began passing items to Wade one by one as he announced his findings.

"Let's see here, we have what appears to be a turkey and ham sandwich." The sandwich found itself to Wade's meaty hands and then carelessly out of Wade's meaty hands and into the sloppy, muddy snow. "A thing of applesauce - Motts, it would appear." The applesauce came open upon contact with the ground, where it fell next to what used to be a perfectly good turkey and ham sandwich. "Dinosaur fruit snacks," Evan listed. Wade opened the packet, ate a blue triceratops, and threw the rest one by one at Eugene, who was still on his back. Each fruit snack hit him in the face, and each one made a swear word come out of his mouth. "And a Capri-Sun. That's what a butt eats for lunch. That's what goes into a sphincter mouth at butt lunch."

"Come on, man! That's made from one hundred percent fruit!"

"You're one hundred percent fruit," Evan said as he passed the juice pouch to Wade. Wade then held it about two feet over Wes's head and squeezed it until it popped, spraying the sticky beverage all the fuck over.

"Oh wait, we also have one Rice Krispy-Treat."

Wade tore the package open, took a big bite, spit it on the ground and threw the rest of it into the pile that was supposed to be today's lunch. Wes's attitude turned from annoyed acceptance to disgusted anxiety as he heard the zipper on the front of Evan's pants being unzipped. The tinkling sound of water hitting objects of various textures and densities seemed to go on for hours until it was finally broken by Eugene's voice calling Evan a *gross twat.*

"There," Evan proudly announced, not the least bit phased at the strangely out of place insult directed at him. "Now it's a turkey and piss sandwich, with a side of ap-piss sauce and dino-piss snacks."

"And a rice-pissy treat for dessert," Wade triumphantly added.

"I get it. Because you pissed all over my lunch," Wes said emotionlessly. "You undoubtedly planned this for a long time. Pretty clever."

"Yeah, we're clever!" Wade screamed into Wes's face. "You know why? Because we're eleven and you're nine. You will never be older than us."

Even held his hand up to Wade, which received a high-five. The two proudly exited the scene, each shoving Wes's shoulder as they walked away. Wes stood there looking at the food on the ground covered in steaming, bright yellow stink liquid.

"Evan should be drinking more water," he said to Eugene as he grabbed his hand to help pull Eugene to his feet. A small girl approached holding a book.

"I don't know why you let them bother you, Wesley,"

"Why I let them? They pissed on my lunch, Bonnie. You're right, I should have tied his wiener in a knot."

"They're just bullies. They're jealous of you. That's all."

"Jealous? Of my pissed-on lunch? You're absolutely right. How could they not be?"

"I don't know why you're getting mad at me," Bonnie decreed.

"I'm not mad at you, Bonnie. I'm mad with you," Wes said, knowing full well that what he said wasn't a thing.

"That's not a thing, Wesley."

Wes, Bonnie and Eugene all turned their attention to the gross pile of food, urine, white and yellow snow, and mud. What they became aware of that had not been there a second ago was the large, looming shadow slowly encompassing the mess. They looked at each other, exchanging expressions of dread.

"Wes. Did you make this mess?" The voice that these words were made out of was older and low. It was the kind of voice that belonged to someone who was over fifty-years-old but had somehow smoked seventy-year's-worth of cigarettes, and it was familiar.

"No, Ms. Caldwell, I didn't dump out my own lunch and pee all over it."

"But you admit it's your lunch?" she croaked. "That's your California Raisins lunch box."

Ms. Caldwell had been the recess attendant at this particular elementary school for probably a thousand years. And she sucked. She was mean, violent, and she reeked of every kind of smoke one could imagine. She was only taller than the students by about a foot, even with her tan orthopedic shoes giving her a slight boost and her large, puffy yellow hair.

"Yes, that's my lunchbox and food all over the ground, but I--"

"Do you know, young man, that there are plenty of starving children in the world that would love a turkey sandwich?" she asked him as her voice got scratchier. "Even if it has a little piss on it!"

"No one is that starving. But if you want me to, I'll mail that peed-on sandwich to Uganda."

Ms. Caldwell looked at Wes for a moment, deciding what to say to his smart statement. She must not have found the right words because instead of a verbal response, she quickly reached out to Wes's face and gave him two quick slaps; front and back-hand.

"Oh, shit dick!" are the words that tumbled out of Eugene's mouth at the sight of this.

"Watch your mouth, you little bastards!" she coughed as she pushed Eugene in the chest with the intent to knock him on his butt, which is exactly what happened. "Now, you listen here, Wes," she said looking increasingly sinister. "Somebody needs to teach you a lesson about picky eating. There is not enough food in the world to waste it."

She bent at a perfect ninety-degree angle, keeping her legs straight and her table-like posterior protruding. She reached for the sandwich and to everyone's disgust, picked it up. The once white bread was now grey and yellow and sopping

12

wet. The turkey, ham, and lettuce were already spilling, sliding out easily with the help of extra mayonnaise. Plop. One by one, all of the children within a hundred feet stopped playing and stared.

"Eat your lunch, Wes, or I'm writing you up a pink slip!" There was an audible gasp from the still-gathering audience.

"You... want me to eat that?"

"I want you to *not waste food!*" she shouted as she forcefully pushed the sloppy pile of shame into his hand.

"I'm pretty sure this is poison now." Wes said while trying to figure out if he should be amused or terrified. There was no way the recess lady expected him to eat this ex-sandwich.

"*Obviously no one has taught you,*" by now she was a mere inch from his face, "*to not waste food! So you're not going to waste this!* Eat the goddamned sandwich or I'll have you and your little bitch buddies written up!"

Bonnie clutched her book tightly to her chest as she briskly walked away avoiding eye-contact with anyone. Wes watched Bonnie peace the fuck out while wondering what she had to worry for. Eugene, on the other hand, was a pink slip away from suspension; mostly for foul language and one incident involving accidentally getting his penis out in front of the girl with Downs Syndrome. He hadn't intended to. His plan was to show it to a stray cat that was skulking around the

13

raspberry bush. As he got closer, he noticed the bees' nest nearby and quickly turned around to run away from his impending doom. He didn't see Brittany watching him until they were face to face to face. In retrospect, he realized his whole plan had been flawed.

"Well, my day has no chance of getting better, so it might as well get worse," said a defeated Wes.

He held the sandwich up to his face and opened his mouth. He slowly inched it in a couple of inches careful to not touch his teeth or tongue. He could taste the air around the sandwich, which was a mixture of mayonnaise, meat, and urine. The crust of the sandwich grazed the back of his tongue, he shut his eyes, took in a deep breath, and closed his teeth.

*

Wes chewed his sandwich lazily, sloshing it around in his mouth and getting the mashed-up food good and mixed with his saliva. It easily slid down his throat hole with little effort. Wes was now in his early thirties, and this sandwich, he assumed, had never been urinated on. He was at work, which meant he was wearing too tight black suit pants, a too tight white collared shirt, and a too shortly-tied red necktie. On his head, he wore a telephone headset over his curly black hair, which probably should have been cut a few weeks ago if it were on the head of someone who cared about that sort of thing. He was sitting at a desk in a cubicle which doesn't need describing because it was exactly like how everyone pictures a cubicle, always. In a neighboring cube sat a thin man dressed roughly the same. His moppy brown hair was pushed to the side to make room for his blackframed glasses.

"Wes!" he shouted into the neighboring cubicle.

"What, Eugene?"

"Did you watch that video I sent you yet?"

"No, I've been working. What is it?" he said, moving his bite of sandwich into his right cheek as to avoid it hindering his speech.

"It's, well..." Eugene was struggling for the right words. "Fucking," he stalled, "It's this tortoise and he's banging this lady tortoise! I assume anyway, not that I'm judging, I've just never heard of a gay tortoise."

"Banging?" Wes questioned.

"What, you want me to say 'making love?' But it's the craziest thing, the guy tortoise is making this sound like a--" Eugene made a sort of high-pitched wheezing/whining sound by breathing inwardly. He continued, "I can't really do it, but it's amazing! Horny tortoises, right?"

"Horny tortoises: story of my life," Wes mocked as he clicked on the link Eugene emailed him. Sure enough, the video loaded and was exactly what Eugene described.

"You know, for not having at all the same vocal structure as a mid-coitis reptile, you did an amazingly accurate representation of his sound-of-passion."

"I stayed up late practicing," Eugene answered honestly.

"Did you see the video of that--" Wes's sentence was interrupted due to his sandwich being slapped out of his hand by another hand. Said hand was attached to the arm of Lance McGrott, Wes's boss.

"What did I tell you about eating in your workspace, Wes?!" Lance asked without at all trying to hide his anger and hatred for Wes.

"That it's absolutely okay and everyone does it always?" Wes replied without at all giving a shit.

"You don't," Lance said adjusting his pink tie.

He wasn't as tall as Wes but luckily Wes was sitting down allowing Lance to menacingly tower above him. Wes always thought Lance kind of looked like the guy who played Scott Baio's buddy on Charles In Charge but didn't remember his name; the actor's or the character's.

"Your dumb gross face makes me want to throw up right on it. That way I have something else to look at other than your dumb gross face. When there's also food going into that head-hole of yours--"

"Fine. I'll finish my lunch in my car," Wes said starting to stand up.

"Before he drives it to the corner where your mom works!" Eugene shouted from the other side of the wall.

"You mean your piece of shit Honda Civic that you parked in front of the loading zone sign that I had towed an hour ago?"

"We don't have a loading zone, sir," Wes pointed out confused.

"We do as of an hour ago, and your car was blocking it! Come on Wes, keep up with company policy if you value your job."

"No one values this shit!" Eugene shouted again from his desk, through a mouth-full of Arby's curly fries.

Lance ignored the comment, unwilling to break eye contact with Wes. For what felt like an hour but was probably more like a full minute, they stared at each other. Neither knew what the next move would be. Finally, as if to break the silent tension, Lance pushed everything that was on Wes's desk onto the floor. The sound arose Eugene's curiosity enough to stand on his chair and look over the wall. Neither Wes nor Eugene expected Lance to unzip his fly, untuck his member, and with both hands back on his hips, pee on the pile of Wes's things. Eugene was angry on behalf of Wes, yet impressed with Mr. McGrott for being able to pee in front of them with such ease. Wes sat motionless, staring where up until a few seconds ago his computer screen had been.

"Horny tortoises," he said out loud to no one.

CHAPTER 1: The First Chapter

Wes sat alone in his apartment. He took the last sip of his Pabst Blue Ribbon and mindlessly threw the can near a pile of other cans. The couch where he was sitting was old and worn out when he got it. He had a suspicion that nobody had ever purchased the couch new and it had somehow just been passed on and on since the dawn of time. He moved his feet off of the cooler they were propped up on in place of a coffee table. His television set was blaring a soccer game. Wes didn't care much for *sport*, but he liked soccer because watching it made him feel European. He also had a great time imagining the little black and white ball being kicked around turning into the heads of people he knew. That made him feel good inside.

Next to the couch was a chair that frankly didn't match anything else in his small apartment. It was angled toward the TV. Wes opened the cooler in front of him and reached for another can of Pabst, pausing momentarily to consider reaching for the bottle of Old Grandad whiskey that was also in the cooler. *Whiskey is a social drink*, he thought to himself. He figured only alcoholics drink whiskey by themselves, and he was no alcoholic. He was just enjoying his seventh can of Pabst. The sound of popping open the can was not loud enough to block the sound of someone knocking on his door. *This will*, he thought as he grabbed the remote from the couch cushion next to him and cranked the volume on the television. After a few seconds, the knocking sounded again. Wes, again, countered this by turning up the TV.

"You're a dick," shouted Eugene from the other side of the door.

"You're a dick," Wes said back, without taking his eyes off of the soccer game. Eugene briefly considered kicking the door in, but thought he might try turning the door knob first. The door opened. *Next time*, he thought.

Eugene sauntered into the apartment right up to Wes, snatched the can of beer out of Wes's hand, and took a healthy gulp before Wes could even get his first sip. Eugene sat down next to Wes on the worn-out couch with his newly-claimed beverage. Wes held up his middle finger as he got another beer out of the cooler. Eugene grinned from behind the can that was up to his mouth. They sat staring at the soccer game silent and motionless, aside from the occasional sips and burps. A half hour passed without being noticed.

"Should we get a pizza?" Eugene said without changing his glance.

There was no response and the subject was seemingly dropped. Another few minutes went by before there was another knock on Wes's apartment door.

"Pizza got here quick," Wes noted.

"I didn't order one," Eugene said back, matter-of-factly.

"Then holy shit, what's with all the commotion tonight?!" Wes shouted. From the other side of the door came a woman's voice.

"Let me in, Wesley!" she called.

Wes slowly stood up making a huge production out of it, sighing and stretching. He walked across the room to his front door and opened it. Standing in front of him was Bonnie. She started to walk through the doorway but Wes blocked her out like a dick.

"Come on, dude!" she said with a half grin.

"I don't know. So far you haven't given me the password," Wes told her, with absolutely no hint of playfulness in his voice. Bonnie held the six-pack of Pabst she was carrying up in front of Wes's eyes.

"Correct," he told her, stepping aside allowing her to enter his domain.

They walked to the cooler and Wes pushed Eugene's legs off of it giving him access to the inside. He removed a can from Bonnie's six-pack and added the rest of the new beers to the pile of beer, ice, and that bottle of Old Grandad whiskey living inside the light blue and white cooler. He started to close the cooler but again spotted the whiskey, this time seizing it in his hand. Bonnie opened her beer and sat on the other side of the couch leaving a spot for Wes wide open in between herself and Eugene. Wes closed the cooler and looked at both of them, who were both looking at the television screen.

"Why don't either of you ever take the chair?" Wes asked them.

"It's too hard," replied Bonnie.

"It isn't angled at the TV enough," Eugene claimed.

"Fair enough, Goldilocks," Wes said to whoever acknowledged him, which neither did.

He sat down in between them and propped his feet up on the cooler. The other two followed suit. The three of them sat with their feet up, cheers'd their beers together without actually saying *cheers*, and took sips. Wes took a slug from the whiskey bottle and started to pass it to Eugene, but Bonnie snatched it from her side of the couch and took a long pull from it before forcing it into Eugene's hand. Wes grinned but Eugene suppressed his. They silently watched the television and drank. After another fifteen minutes passed, Bonnie burped

"Excuse me," she said covering her mouth.

"Boy, somebody's a real miss fucking chatterbox tonight!" Eugene said, rudely.

"I just said 'excuse me,' cock breath," she said back.

"See? There is is again. Yap, yap, yap!" Eugene said as he mockingly held up his hand, miming a puppet or a duck, nobody was sure which.

Wes, without turning his head, reached his hand over and slapped Eugene in the face. Not very hard, but hard enough to make a point.

"I'm so glad we're best friends, Wesley" Bonnie said sarcastically, but she meant it regardless.

Wes and Bonnie had known each other for nearly twenty-six years. She was the first friend Wes ever made at school, purely by coincidence. They had randomly been seated next to each other on their first day of kindergarten. Another boy in their class made fun of Bonnie's glasses until tears came out from behind them. Wes didn't say anything to the boy or come to her defense in any way, but later he drew a crude picture of the boy eating excrement coming straight out of the anus of a horse. Bonnie laughed at that crayon drawing harder than an average six-year-old girl should have until the teacher came to see what was so funny. Wes got scolded, and the other boy got nothing. Wes didn't know it yet, but that was to be a running theme in his life.

As close as they were, Wes never questioned or corrected her constant addressing him as *Wesley*. He wondered if she thought his first name was Wesley. But he was pretty sure she knew his last name was Westin. Did she think his name was Wesley Westin? Whatever the case, it had gone on for much too long for him to question it now. To her, he was and would always be Wesley, and he wouldn't have it any other way. Besides, it had been so long since anyone called him Michael that he had the tendency to forget that that was his proper name.

Bonnie was no longer an awkward little four-eyed girl, though still donning glasses. She was a little taller than Eugene and slightly thick in the places that counted, giving her prominent curves. She had always been on the voluptuous side, but became more so after having a son seven years ago. In high school she got picked on for having large breasts for her age. She felt bad about this until Eugene once pointed out that making fun of a girl for having *huge jugs* was like *teasing someone for having too much money, or giving shit to a chef who made food taste too good. And it didn't make any god damn sense!* Wes didn't agree or disagree, instead he turned red,

24

which was how he usually reacted when Bonnie's gender was pointed out. He was more comfortable thinking about her as a guy, or some asexual entity in a curly, blonde wig that existed for the sole purpose of companionship.

"Fuck you both," Wes finally responded to Bonnie's sentiment as they touched the top edges of their cans together.

That was the last thing that was said out loud until there was yet another knock at the door. Wes's face accurately reflected the combination of confusion, rage, worry, and apprehension he was feeling inside his body. He involuntarily dented his beer can by clutching it tightly.

"You think that's somebody to piss all over your shit?" Eugene mocked.

"If it is, let's hope your face gets hit as an innocent bystander," Wes answered as he slammed the rest of his beverage. "Seriously, I don't know who the fuck that could be except bad news, like ninjas or something. I'll be under my bed."

"Relax, ladies. It's probably the pizza I ordered," Bonnie said smugly.

"I didn't hear you order a pizza. *Why would you cover for the ninja outside*?!" Eugene screamed. "Unless you're *one of them*!" He threw his empty beer can at her ribs.

"Pizza app. I can order food without making a call and pay with my thumbprint." Wes and Eugene looked at each other and then at Bonnie. Wes spoke first.

"It's like she's a god damn wizard!"

"Sneaky secret pizza! Holy shit, nailed it!" Eugene added.

Wes answered the door, which had been knocked on again. The pizza guy started to speak, but Wes snatched the pizza from him and slammed the door in his face.

"All hail Pizza Wizard!"

He brought the pizza to the others, kicked their feet off of the cooler, and placed the pizza box on it. They dug in, grabbing a slice each, cheese and sauce slopping over the edge of the cardboard container and onto the cooler.

"Why didn't you conjure up some bread sticks?" Eugene asked dickishly. Bonnie responded by showing him the huge wad of chewed-up pizza in her mouth. "And maybe some manners?" He added at the sight of this. Bonnie and Wes giggled.

"Well gentlemen, and I use that term incredibly loosely," Bonnie started, "It's almost time for me to pick up Jeremy."

"Has he made any friends at school yet?" Wes asked of her little boy.

"I mean..." It appeared as though her face was starting to say and then abandon several words before she found an appropriate one. "No." she settled with. "Not yet," she added hopefully.

"Is that because he's a little shit-eating bastard?" Eugene politely questioned.

"He doesn't eat shit!" Bonnie reminded him. "But some jerk at school made him eat sand out of the sandbox."

"Classic," Wes noted.

"I called the little prick's parents, but they didn't seem to give any shits."

"Nah, They never do. Usually, somebody who is enough of an asshole to behave like that will never learn a lesson from their parents anyway. Or their teachers, for that matter."

"The only language they know is that of bruises and knuckles!" Eugene triumphantly added as he went for another slice of pizza.

"I considered taking some legal action, but I don't want Jeremy to seem even more like a pussy. Right? I feel like that's a bitch move, to bring the law into it. Does that make him, and by extension me, so us," her logic was flawless, "does that make us pussies?"

Wes and Eugene nodded unapologetically.

27

"Speaking of your pussy, is Jeremy still at his dad's house?" Wes suddenly appeared to have taken a deep interest in the toppings on his pizza, as his gaze was suddenly buried in his dinner. Bonnie looked at Eugene and again, struggled momentarily to find the right words.

"Yes."

Wes couldn't tell if the tension was broken or rising, until Eugene let out one gleeful laugh as Bonnie truthfully answered his question.

"Bonnie, can I ask you a question? And don't say 'duh you just asked one uh-duh' because everyone who says shit like that should be thrown off a building," Wes meandered from his query.

"Duh, what's your question, Dummy?" she asked him first.

"When Jeremy was being made," Bonnie's suddenly sharp look interrupted Wes's question. "I mean, grown; when he was growing inside you, not like when he was being *made* made..." Wes accompanied the end of his sentence with a gesture comprised of his index finger going in and out of a circle made with his opposing index finger and thumb.

"Go on," she said, intrigued, not yet knowing whether or not she should start getting offended.

"Did you ever consider marrying him? You know, make an honest man out of him?

"What? No!" Bonnie replied surprised. Replised. "I thought he was gay right up until his dick was inside me! Joke's on me, right? Or in me, I guess."

"You love dicks in you." Eugene made clear what he was taking away from the conversation. "When are you going to let Wes put his goldenrod in your treasure box?"

Wes immediately punched Eugene in the shoulder. Hard.

"Oww! Fuck my cock!" Eugene swore as he rubbed his shoulder. "God dammit Wes, why don't you throw punches like that around the office? Your stuff would probably stop getting peed on." Bonnie gave Wes a concerned look. He nodded as if to say, *Yeah my stuff got peed on again. Please don't make me explain further.*

"For the same reason I never fought back in school: it seems like fighting back would just prolong the shit-storm. If I don't react, they'll get bored and leave."

"Well it's a good thing that tactic is foolproof or you'd probably still have problems with bullies," Eugene sarcastically pointed out. Wes heard loud and clear what he was saying.

"Okay, fine. It's because they're usually bigger than me. But also the other thing."

"I think it's sweet," Bonnie said. Wes couldn't tell if she was serious or making fun of him. "It's that 'lover, not a fighter' thing." Now Wes was pretty sure she was making fun of him.

"Fuck yeah, I'm sweet! I'm sweet as fuck! So how about letting me put my dick in you now?" Wes's snarky suggestion was answered with a punch in the shoulder from Bonnie, rivaling the one punch Eugene had just received from Wes. "Ouch! The fuck! You better watch it toots! You're not bigger than me! I'll punch you in the god damn mouth if I have to in order to teach you a lesson!" The grin across Eugene's face spread wider than it had been since watching those horny tortoises on the Internet.

"You are a man of honor to teach such lessons." Eugene's bad impression of an old Japanese sensei came across as racist. "But only those ah-much smaller than you are ah-worthy of your wisdom!"

"Yeah, Mickey Rooney," Wes agreed. "Women and children seem to be my target demographic."

"I'm not sure how far I'd advertise that. You might end up on the news," Bonnie advised as she stood up. "Alright bitches. Time to go get Jeremy from his dad's."

"Are you sure you're good to drive after downing that half-a beer and one shot over the course of two hours on a full stomach?" Eugene asked deadpan. "Little miss party animal," he added to further his point.

30

Bonnie, who had turned toward the door across the room, put her middle finger in the air and kept it there until she was out the door and it was closed behind her. Wes and Eugene polished off the pizza over the course of a couple more beers and random glugs of Old Grandad. The soccer game had ended and the news was on, because one of them was sitting on the remote and they neither cared who or to get up.

"Man." Wes sighed. "It's a drag Jeremy is getting picked on at school. That kid doesn't have a chance."

"A chance at what? Not being an outcast? All the cool kids are outcasts." Eugene noted.

"No, the cool kids are the cool kids. And a chance at defending himself. His dad's a passivist, you remember. Maybe that's why everyone thought he was gay twenty years ago. Either way, he's not going to teach him how to throw a hook."

"Maybe we should teach him karate," suggested Eugene.

"Because we know karate?" Wes questioned.

"You don't?" Eugene asked smugly as the beer can connected with his lips.

"Yeah I'm sweet as fuck of course I know karate! But legally I'm not allowed to show my advanced moves to minors. Although maybe for his birthday we could buy him karate lessons or something. I don't know. I don't like him getting beat up like we did every day."

31

"Come on, Wes. That's just how it works. It's almost like a rite of passage or something. It's as much a part of school as Social Studies."

"Ha. 'Social Studies'," Wes repeated amusedly. "The fuck was up with that shit, right?"

"Yeah that wasn't anything," Eugene concluded. "But getting shit on, you and I went through it. Bonnie went through it. God damn, the only person who didn't get picked on at school was probably that fucktard from your work. And that's only because he was doing the picking."

Wes frowned. The thought of a ten-year-old Lance McGrott throwing rocks at Bonnie's little boy entered his mind. He winced at the thought. Then present-day Lance McGrott entered the picture bitch-slapping his ten-year-old counterpart. Imaginary ten-year-old Lance fell down and started crying. Wes smiled satisfactorily, but his face changed to concern after a couple seconds.

"But that's a paradox!" he said louder than he meant to.

"Have some more whiskey, Ol' Grandad," Eugene replied, not seeming surprised at what just came out of Wes's mouth.

"I just... It's too bad schools don't employ a designated bully stopper," Wes said as he thought.

"Isn't that was the recess aid is supposed to do?" Eugene and Wes both shuddered, accidentally thinking of Ms. Caldwell. "Mushroomheaded bitch," Eugene muttered about the woman neither of them had seen in over twenty years.

"Okay scratch that. What could a designated bully-stopper possibly do?"

"I dunno, stop the bully maybe?" Wes said in a mocking tone. Eugene held up his middle finger to Wes, and kept it up as he spoke.

"What I mean, genius, is how? Teachers aren't allowed to touch students at all anymore. What would they threaten them with? Detention? Suspension? Bullies love getting suspended. It's their golden ticket. Kick a little bastard out of class? Great, learning is a drag! Call the parents? How the hell do you think they became little bullying bastards in the first place?"

"They could... Fail them?" Wes was starting to wonder about his idea.

"For being mean? Not fucking likely. And even if they were allowed to, that's just keeping the hypothetical little shit around school longer. No. To stop a bully, one would have to physically beat them down. And no school would allow that." Eugene had a point, but the wheels in Wes's head were still turning.

"But don't you remember Evan Thomas? Think about how awesome it would have been if somebody would have taken our side. Somebody big enough to take him out and then be all, 'You're safe from now on, Kid. Go play on the merry-go-round in peace.'"

"You mean like if Batman lived on our playground instead of Gotham City? Yeah, of course that would have ruled. But it's a fucking fantasy. In the real world, mean kids take every opportunity to shit on nice kids. That's just how the hierarchy of the playground works. Since the dawn of time. *The dawn of time!*" Eugene said as he slammed his empty beer can dramatically onto the cooler.

"Yeah, I know. And it sucks. But if I had a time machine, I'd go back and knock the living shit out of eleven-year-old Evan Thomas." Wes's fist clenched as the name rolled off his tongue.

Eugene gasped at the sound of his name.

"Oh come on, it's not like I said Lord Voldemort," Wes said noticing Eugene's reaction.

"Well it's not like you-know-who didn't deserve a beat down by some stranger in his thirties," Eugene said.

Those words repeated over and over in Wes's head. *It's not like Evan Thomas didn't deserve a beat down by some stranger in his thirties.* What was it about this statement that sent him so deep into his own mind? Through the haze of Pabst and whiskey, Wes was slowly but surely on his way to an idea. He dug the remote out from under his left butt cheek and clicked off the television, turned is whole body toward Eugene, and looked him right in the face. Eugene looked back, first by just moving his eyes. His head followed.

"Um, if you're going to make out with me, I'm going to need more beer," Eugene said calmly.

"Shut up and hear me out!" Wes snapped. He needed to focus if he was going to verbalize the feeling he was feeling. "When we were nine, we couldn't beat up Evan Thomas because he was eleven. But, now we're not nine."

"You did it!" Eugene congratulated Wes. "Except," he continued, "that Evan Thomas is still older than us. Do you want to track him down and face him as adults?" There was momentary silence before he continued further. "Because I bet we still can't beat him up as adults."

Wes looked at Eugene. Eugene wasn't getting the point. What even was his point?

"No, no. You're not listening. Jeremy can't beat up whoever is picking on him at school because he's younger and smaller. But I bet when he's a grown-up, he'll want to have a time machine to come back and beat up this jerk. Like what we want right now. The emotions we are feeling *right fucking now* are exactly what he's going to feel in twenty-three years."

"Well of course, Wes! Everyone wants a time machine!" Eugene correctly assessed. "By the way, are you picturing something like a laser device that shoots you through time or a DeLorean?"

"Don't be a fucking idiot. Of course, a DeLorean. But that's not the point." Wes paused to consider how to address his next point. "This is: we are here now."

"Can't argue with that logic!" Eugene happily said popping open yet another beer.

"We live in Jeremy's hometown. We live in his childhood. And we don't work for the school. We," Wes paused for effect, "could teach this bully a lesson." His eyes widened at Eugene like a stray dog finding a full steak on the sidewalk.

"Um... this seems like a bad idea." Eugene wasn't sure if Wes was kidding or not. He didn't look kidding. Because he wasn't.

"In what way?" Wes's speech became more passionate. "You *just* said that the only thing that would take out a bully is a beat-down. And you just said how much it sucked getting picked on every day. And you *just said* that I could currently totally beat up an eleven-year-old!" Eugene nodded in agreement about the last part.

"Wes. This is a fun scenario and all. But it's usually a bad choice to beat up kids, even if they have it coming."

"Bullshit! We won't get caught. We'll hide out on the playground, put on a disguise, and stop the bullies!" It was all starting to make sense now to Wes. "What's the main reason we don't fight crime, Eugene?"

"We are weak and could get shot and killed."

"Exactly! But we are fucking tough as shit compared to schoolchildren!" Wes's face was beaming. Eugene stared blankly at Wes. A moment passed as Eugene sipped his adult beverage and thought.

"You know, maybe it's the beer talking, but suddenly I am one-hundred-percent behind this idea," he finally said without at all changing his expression.

Wes lit up. His mouth curled into a devious smile as he spoke.

"We're gonna need costumes."

CHAPTER 2: Thrifty Business

Bonnie's car rolled effortlessly into the driveway of an average sized brick house downtown. The lights stayed on for a few seconds after she'd shut off the vehicle and exited. It was dusk, the sun was nearly set. She looked right at the sunset for a second before wincing and wondering why she'd looked right into the sun. She looked back to the door. It was hazy but rematerialized in front of her eyes as her vision adjusted. She knocked. The sound of a man getting up and walking toward the door went into her ears.

As the door opened, she saw a tall, thin thirty-something gentleman wearing argyle socks, khaki pants, and a white collared shirt under a light blue cardigan. As he pulled the door toward him, he attempted to push his short, brown hair off of his forehead but it remained exactly where it was before due to the amount of styling product keeping it in place.

"Hi, Gary!" Bonnie said cheerily.

"Hi, Bonnie," he returned. "Come on in." She walked past him and entered the house. As he followed, she looked back and spoke to him.

"Is Jeremy ready to go yet?" she asked.

"Just about. Figure skating is going to end in a few minutes."

She found her son sitting on the couch, eyes glued to the sixty-five inch television hanging on the wall. She sat next to him and gave him a hug, which he excitedly returned.

"Mommy! You just missed the Axel jump!" Jeremy said to his mother, who smiled. They watched the two skaters finish their routine. Once they were done and bowing to the crowd, Bonnie stood up.

"Come on, buddy. Let's get you to bed. Did you have a good day?"

As she asked him this question, she grabbed his arm and pulled it toward her, gesturing to stand up. Jeremy jolted and shouted.

"*Ouch! Mom!*"

"Oh, I'm sorry, sweetie, I didn't mean to grab you so hard!"

"Oh," Gary reluctantly interrupted. "You probably didn't grab him any harder than your should have. He just has quite a bruise there, from some student hitting him." Gary's face went cold.

"Did you tell a teacher?" Bonnie asked Jeremy, trying not to overreact.

"He said he'd do it again harder if I told," Jeremy replied, dejectedly.

"Do you know his name?" Bonnie asked. Jeremy's brow furrowed.

"It was Jake Mortinburg! He's a fifth-grader."

"And why was he hitting you?"

"Because," he started excitedly, "because he wanted my markers! The ones you bought me for school are better than the ones he has and he wanted to take mine but I told him 'no!'"

"I'm glad you told him 'no.' They're your markers and he doesn't have any right to take them. Come on now, let's get in the car and get you to bed. What you need is a good sleep. It will make you feel better," Bonnie told Jeremy, and herself.

"I felt better before you grabbed my fucking arm!"

Gary gasped at the word that came out of his son's mouth.

"Don't," Bonnie put on her serious voice, "say that word in front of me." Gray looked bewildered at her. "Or ever!" she quickly added. "Have a good night, Gary. Thanks for showing him sports."

"You too, Hun," Gary said. He then crouched down in front of Jeremy bringing them eye to eye. He said to his son softly, "Bye, little buddy. Don't let those awful older boys get to you. If you stoop to their primitive level of antagonizing violently, they win."

Gary stood back up and patted Jeremy on the head as Bonnie took Jeremy by the hand and led him out the door. Bonnie unlocked her car with the click of a button on her keychain. She helped Jeremy into his car seat behind her hers and he buckled himself. She walked around and got behind the wheel. She put the key in the ignition and started the car, but didn't immediately put her vehicle in gear.

"Sweetie, can I ask you a question?" she asked while looking at him through the rear-view mirror.

"You just did!" Jeremy responded and giggled. Bonnie wished Wes could have heard that. She thought it was ironic, but it wasn't. It was coincidence.

"Do you still like watching the skate-dancing on TV?" she asked.

"Yeah, it's real neat!" Jeremy replied. Bonnie took a moment to consider her next move. She wanted to be delicate but understood. She breathed heavy before speaking again.

"You know, it's okay to be different, right? If you start to feel like you're different from most other people you know, that's okay. Better than okay! Mommy and Daddy - especially Daddy! Well, no, both of us equally - we will always love you no matter what. No matter who you choose to be." She thought about what she'd just said and added "Not that it's a choice! I just--"

"I know, Mom, don't get mushy. And also, when they go real fast on their ice skates and turn, you can see right up the ladies' skirts! And sometimes they just hold their leg right up! So everyone can see pretty much everything!"

"I should have known," Bonnie said with a smile.

"And when the tall men put their legs straight out, you can see the shape of their balls!"

Bonnie put the car in reverse, backed out of the driveway, and headed home.

*

A few aisles into a local thrift store, two men flipped through clothing racks. They either didn't notice or didn't care that they were receiving plenty of odd looks from the young, tattooed girl behind the counter. This may very well have been because it was almost closing time and they were the only ones in the store. It may also have been their loud, swear-filled muttering about harming children. Either way, she had already decided she would not be sleeping with either of them. Probably. She was a particularly easy slut, after all. She brushed her dyed-black hair off of her black-framed glasses and watched Wes put on a black ski-mask, get spit on it, take it off and put it back in a spot that was nowhere close to where he had picked it up. She tried hard not to listen but heard Wes address Eugene anyway.

"Do you even remember what time recess was?"

"Are you kidding? That's like the only thing I remember. Aside from the fact that sometimes for lunch the choice was between triangle pizza and square pizza." Wes pictured the cafeteria lunch choice in his mind. It had never occurred to him how odd of an option that was.

"I just," Wes started before pausing to think. "I don't know how long we should hide out on the playground. I mean, I only have an hour break for lunch and I usually take it around twelve-thirty.

"Dude, recess was at nine forty-five. Is that too early for your lunch break?"

"Considering I get there at nine o'clock, sharp?" Eugene gave Wes a smarmy look at his preposterous statement. Wes continued, "Okay, 9:15 sharp. But the point is, we need to come up with an excuse other than 9:30 lunch break to get out of work."

"Ferris Bueller would build a dummy of himself and rig tape recorders so that when he left, no one would be the wiser," Eugene excitedly and drunkenly told Wes.

"Ferris Bueller would talk his fucked-up friend Cameron into slicing this kid head-to-toe with a box-cutter while he butt-fucked Sloan Peterson on the hood of Principal Rooney's car." The girl behind the counter looked up upon hearing Wes's statement. The combination of a Ferris Bueller reference and anal intercourse made her quite horny indeed. Slut.

"Hey, check this out!" Eugene exclaimed to Wes as he held up a pin-striped three-piece suit.

"Shit bitch, I don't know a couple of muthafuckas more gangsta than us!"

Hearing Wes say that sentence suspended any arousal that was still lingering in the check-out girl's nether regions. Eugene put on the jacket of the suit and buttoned it over his clothes. Wes nodded approvingly, grinning at Eugene. "We should probably get masks though."

"What are those bank-robbing masks called?" Eugene wondered aloud.

"I'm sure they're actually called 'bank-robbing' masks," Wes snarked back, "and I just saw some over here." Wes gestured for Eugene to follow him to the ski-masks. They each took one and put it on, stretching them all the way on to conceal their faces.

"We. Look. Awesome." Wes stated dramatically.

"Yeah," Eugene half agreed as his eyes jumped to something across the aisle, "but we could do with a little more awesome..."

He trailed off as he walked toward the thing that so suddenly and completely captured his attention. Wes watched as Eugene picked up a black fedora with a feather in the brim and held it victoriously in the air. He lowered it onto his head, which was still covered by a black ski-mask.

"Holy fuck, dude. That's it!" Wes was taking it all in, just how the girl behind the counter often did. Wes looked over the dark jacket, face mask and hat. "That's so fucking scary and pimp, which isn't a word I just throw around." Wes thought for a moment before saying, "You look like," he thought about his words carefully, "Like if black people had their own Ku Klux Klan but in reverse. That's how they would dress to lynch whities."

"I always thought regular Ku Klux Klan members dressed like assholes. You know if black people had their own they'd look awesome doing it," Eugene agreed.

45

None of this was what the girl behind the counter expected to hear tonight.

"You know how we're gonna look?" Eugene asked Wes.

Eugene mimed a gangster pulling a tommy gun out from his jacket and proceeded to shoot an imaginary wall of people with it. He then threw down his air-gun and mimicked pulling two glocks out from the front of his pants, cocked them sideways, and silently shot the bodies on the floor one by one in the head. Wes's genuine smile of excitement slowly transformed into a fake, broad grimace as he didn't know whether or not to be impressed or terrified. The girl behind the counter chose to be impressed because she was into *bad boys*.

"There are two of those hats, right?" Wes asked.

Eugene threw his two pretend handguns onto the imaginary bodies, spit real spit at them, grabbed an identical hat and tossed it to Wes.

"Good. Let's buy this stuff, go home, and drink ourselves to sleep so we wake up good and pissed off. We'll meet at the school at 9:00." He stopped to think again. "Maybe I'll just call in to work altogether. It's not like I can get a lot done with my shit in a big pee-pile."

"You know, I think worrying about how to get out of work is the kind of thing pussies who don't beat up schoolchildren do. But not us!" They both laughed.

The girl behind the counter could not hide the look that spread across her face like a man's climax so often did. Wes and Eugene both saw her look of alarm and for the first time became aware that she may have heard them say something suspicious. Eugene quickly covered for them.

"Oh don't worry. These kids totally have it coming," he said as he punched the palm of his hand with his other hand.

"Hey, speaking of which," Wes said without finishing.

On the other end of town, a cellular telephone was sitting silently on a nightstand. Next to the phone was a lamp, which was not turned on, a tissue box, and a clock radio. Next to the nightstand was a bed containing a curly blonde-haired woman wearing glasses and a white tank-top. She was looking at the television, which was turned on with the volume down very low. The glow from the television basked everything in the room with soft, blue flickering light. Her phone began to buzz on the wooden top of the nightstand. She reached over and picked it up. The screen gave no doubts as to who was calling her.

"What do you want, Wesley?" Bonnie asked. The words of her statement expressed more annoyance than the inflection with which they were said.

"Hey, what's the name of that prick who was beating up Jeremy?" Wes's voice said through her phone speaker.

"Oh. Uhm, let's see. I think he said it was Jake something..."

"Jake something? That isn't good enough. Give me his *full name*." Wes meant business.

"Well," Bonnie started as she thought, "Jeremy just told me what his name was when we were at his Dad's house earlier. He has a big, fresh bruise on his arm from the little shit."

Bonnie's words went into her phone's microphone where they were digitally converted into ones and zeros, beamed into outer space where they were collected by satellites and transmitted back to Earth into Wes's phone, where they shot out of his phone's speaker and into his ears like anger-bullets hitting his brain.

"Mother. Fuck." Wes responded as his face went pink from his blood rising.

"Mortinburg! Kid's name is Jake Mortinburg," Bonnie blurted out as she remembered. She suddenly realized she didn't know why on earth Wes would need his name. "Wait! Why on earth do you need his name?" She also blurted out as her brain processed information. "Are you going to call his parents or something?"

"Or something," Wes said as low and intimidating as he could make his voice go.

"Click."

There was silence until Bonnie broke it.

"Why did you say 'click?'" she finally asked. "Was that you pretending to hang up?" Wes didn't answer, but she could tell that he was still on the line. "I can hear you breathing, creep. Is your mouth open?"

"I thought that would be a dramatic place to end the call, but I'm not ready to actually get off the phone yet," Wes explained.

"Well what else do you need? I'm in bed."

"Oh you're in bed?" Wes said in a mock-seductive voice. "What are you wearing? Handcuffs?" It wasn't a good one.

"She's in bed?" Eugene asked, having been half-listening the whole time and half trying on cool sunglasses. "Ask if she's handcuffed to it."

"I totally just did!" Bonnie heard Wes say through the phone, followed by the slap of what could only be a high-five.

"Hey Boner Brothers, I can still hear you," she reminded them, not that they would behave any differently.

"Right," Wes replied, abruptly ceasing his giggle fit with Eugene. "Well that's really all I needed I guess."

"What are you guys doing, anyway?" Bonnie asked, curiously. Eugene clearly heard this question through Wes's phone.

"Your Mom!" Eugene shouted toward the phone, ensuring that Bonnie could hear his awesome and hilarious response on her end. That was a good one. Wes gave him an approving nod before giving his own answer.

"That's for us to know. Click." There was another moment of silence before Bonnie spoke up.

"Did you just say 'click' again?"

"Yeah, but this time I'm really getting off the phone. Night, Buddy."

"Night, poobs."

Poob was a word that Wes, Eugene, and Bonne added to their lexicon when they found it on the internet. Someone had included this magical word in a comment under a YouTube video. It was clearly the misspelling of the word *pube*, but pronouncing it *poob* brought the three of them into hysterical laughter whenever it was said aloud. Their call ended as Wes burst into a short, but prominent laugh.

"She called us 'poobs,'" he said to Eugene, who gave a laugh-shout. They brought their stuff to the checkout girl, who wordlessly scanned everything. If Eugene hadn't known any better, he'd have sworn she was staring right at the crotch of his jeans. After the girl rang up their purchases, she spoke in a monotone voice that would impress a robot. Not a new robot, but like a 1920s Fritz Lang Metropolis robot. A new robot would not be impressed in the least.

"So. Two black three-piece suits, two ski-masks..."

"Ski masks!" both of the men interrupted in unison, remembering what those hats were called. The girl continued.

"Two fedora hats, two pairs of black leather gloves," Wes looked at Eugene.

"Nice," he said. Eugene must have picked those up while he was on the phone. Eugene smiled menacingly.

"And one white tee-shirt clearly showcasing how much coffee Garfield requires to survive Mondays." Wes gave Eugene a look of confusion and disgust. Eugene smiled innocently, shrugging.

"Your total comes to $9 dollars," the girl finally finished.

"This place is fucking awesome," Wes said as he handed her a $10 dollar bill. The girl took it and gave him a dollar back.

"Have fun murdering children," she said. There was no grin on her face but it was implied. Wes and Eugene laughed like she was an idiot.

"We're not going to *murder* them!" Wes exclaimed as they continued their laughter, which stopped suddenly as Eugene continued Wes's thought.

"But we do want to bring them as close to death as possible. Can we have a bag?"

The girl handed Eugene a large plastic bag and Wes stuffed their purchases into it and started toward the door.

"Thanks, Janeane Garofalo from Reality Bites," Eugene said over his shoulder as they walked outside. Once the door closed behind them, Wes turned excitedly to Eugene.

"Dude, she totally *did* look like Janeane Garofalo from Reality Bites!" Wes happily pointed out.

"Right?!" Eugene said.

And low it was written, there would be but one more high-five exchanged this very nigh, but one alone. For dawning the morrow, t'would be their plan forsooth.

*

The sun shone brightly on an old, brick building which was used as an elementary school. In the bright sunlight, it was easy to see just how old this structure was. The brown bricks looked like they could crumble at any second and there were clear silhouettes of the ivy vines that once climbed the building but were long since dead. In the road in front of the building stood two men, dressed in pin-striped suits, white collared-shirts, black neck ties, black ski-masks over their faces, feather-brimmed fedora hats, and long black capes.

"The capes were a necessary touch," Wes told Eugene. "Where did you get them?"

"From the cape store, who gives a shit?" Eugene was hung-over and annoyed. Wes was also hung-over, but his adrenaline was keeping him upright for the time being.

"Should we plan our attack or just wing it?" Wes questioned Eugene, who was squinting with his hand shielding the sunlight from his face.

"I think that prick sun made it extra bright today just to fuck us! *Fuck you, the sun!*" Eugene was hung-over and annoyed.

"Hey!" Wes was serious. "Don't you *ever* trash-talk the sun in front of me! You should fucking worship it and its gravity for pulling star shit together so we can be here right now to bitch-slap some manners into a little kid!" Eugene couldn't tell if Wes was joking. "That said," Wes went on, "it is bright. We might need sunglasses."

"I bet they have those at the Speedway station on the corner," Eugene suggested.

Wes nodded and they ran as fast as they could, which was not very, one block away to the nearby gas station. Eugene waited outside to keep watch, whatever that meant, while Wes pulled off his ski mask and entered the facility. Wes grabbed two identical pairs of generic, horn-rimmed sun glasses and brought them hurriedly to the counter. There was a happy European man behind the counter. Greek or something.

"It's so bright out you need two pairs, yes?" the man said with a grin.

"Yep, that's exactly right. You got it," Wes agreed as he handed the man a $20 dollar bill.

"You and your friend going to costume party?" the man asked through his thick Greek or something accent. He could see Eugene through the front window. "You Blues Brothers? Fat and thin guy dance around in suits?" He was more excited than he should have been. "Sing blues? 'My baby left me?'"

"Right again," Wes said, wanting his change and for the conversation to stop. "We're going to a costume party. At 9:00 o'clock in the morning. On a Tuesday." The man looked at Wes. "In May," Wes added to hammer home his point. A giant smile took the place of the average-sized smile that was already on the man's face.

"Oh! You're an ass hole!"

The name he called Wes was oddly separated clearly into two words. He handed Wes his change. Wes rotated a full one-hundred-eighty degrees and power walked to the door. The man shouted as Wes walked away.

"Have a good time at camp!"

Confused, Wes stopped and gave him one last look before exiting, the door already pushed open slightly.

"Ass hole camp!" the man finished, his wide smile now leaving his face. Wes left the store and handed Eugene his pair of sunglasses.

"It sounded like that guy said 'asshole camp,'" Eugene told Wes.

"Weird," Wes replied as they ran back to the school.

They decided that the best way to wear sunglasses and a ski-mask was to push the frames into the eyeholes of the masks and behind their ears as opposed to over the outside of their covered heads. They agreed that it was the right choice, as now the only visible skin on them was the small opening around their mouths, and this was bad ass as fuck. They crouched slightly as they made their way behind the school and through a small gate into the playground. Crouching did absolutely no good in hiding them.

"Now. We need to be invisible. We don't emerge until the time is right," Wes told Eugene. "Incognito."

There was a perfect spot on the outskirts of the parameter, which consisted of a row of bushes about four feet high in one corner of the playground. Conveniently, there was just enough room between the bushes and the fence behind them for people to hide. This spot also supplied a rather thorough view of the fenced-in area, but there was no good place on the playground in which to see behind the bushes. It was as figuratively close to the literal definition of *invisible* as one could get in this particular area.

Wes and Eugene were standing behind a maple tree. They could be seen by anyone who had at least one working eyeball. They'd been standing there undetected for nearly ten minutes, but this was mostly due to the fact that it wouldn't be recess for another two minutes and the playground was completely vacant. Wes's heart was beating. Eugene was sweating. The time was approaching and Wes was deep in thought. This was it. They were about to avenge thirty-ish years of being picked on.

This wasn't just for Jeremy. This was for anybody who wanted a hero! This was about setting an example. It's not cool to hurt or steal from others who can't defend themselves! This would finally be an answer! Somewhere inside, little Michael Westin was proud of Wes for the honorable thing he and Eugene were about to do. In just a minute, the bell would ring and they would have the chance to stop bullying for good! It's every kid's - *NAY!* - Every *person's* right to live free—

"Or die hard?" Eugene finished Wes's thought for him, as Wes realized he'd been talking out loud.

"I agree," Eugene plainly said. "Little bastard's a prick. Fuck 'im."

"Everything you say is poetry," Wes told Eugene.

The bell rang.

Children poured through the doors as though a dam had burst. Within fifteen seconds, all of the playground equipment was covered in kids. Wes watched like a hawk, studying each kid he put his gaze on. He didn't know what Jake Mortinburg looked like, but figured he'd be pretty easy to spot, being the kid grabbing some smaller kid by the shoulders and then the kid with a stranger's fist in his mouth breaking all of his teeth. *Yes, Jake would be that kid,* he thought.

"Who are you guys?"

CHAPTER 3: Kids Today

Wes and Eugene looked at each other and then straight down. There was a small boy with ginger hair and freckles looking up at them. He was wearing a jean jacket and clutching a stuffed Gonzo from the Muppets. After enough time had passed for the two men to realize what was going on, Eugene finally spoke.

"You can see us?" he asked, having been convinced that they were completely obstructed from sight by the maple tree they were hiding behind.

"Yes, Mister," the boy politely answered. He thought for a moment and it seemed his brain was making some connections. "Wait," he said. "Can nobody else see you? Are you ghosts?"

"Yes," Wes replied without hesitation. "Yes we are ghosts." The boy put his finger in his nose and looked at them both.

"My dog's name is Rex," he finally told them.

"That is a fantastic and fascinating story, but we are kind of in the middle of something." Wes's urgency in his voice was lost on their new friend.

"Is it a game?" the boy asked. "A ghost game? Can I play?" Wes was just about to tell the little boy to scram when something occurred to him.

"Actually, I believe you can play our ghost game." The boy's eyes widened and his face lit up. "Do you know a fella named Jake Mortinburg?"

This name immediately made the boy's facial expression change into the face of someone who was worried. Because he became worried.

"He's an older kid," said the small boy sheepishly. "He doesn't seem nice."

"He isn't nice," Wes validated. "But we're going to try to make him a little nicer. What's your name, buddy?"

"Henry," said Henry.

"Henry, here's how you can help us play our ghost game."

Across the playground, Jeremy was sitting by himself playing with a Transformer toy. Like operating a Rubix Cube, he transformed the toy yellow Mustang into a humanoid robot, which he then made ice-skate around the concrete. He noticed a shadow on the pretend skating rink. It belonged to a blonde, spiky haired boy around the age of eleven. Jeremy's stomach sank.

"Oh good, you found my Transformer, Germ-y," the older boy said to Jeremy. From where Jeremy was sitting, the sun was behind the older boy's head silhouetting him against the sky.

"It's not yours, Jake. It's mine that I got for Easter," Jeremy told him quietly.

"Well there's only one way to tell." Jake picked up his muddy boot and before Jeremy could react, Jake forced it down onto the Transformer, snapping the arms crudely off and sending the head a few feet away.

"Oh, you're right. It isn't mine. I don't have any broken toys."

Jeremy's eyes stung. He didn't want Jake to see him cry but tears were welling in his bottom eyelids whether he wanted them or not. He opened his mouth to say something, or scream something, he wasn't yet sure which, but another boy's voice was heard instead.

"Hey Jake!" Henry shouted from the nearby maple tree. Jake, not used to being addressed by students younger than he was, turned around slowly and annoyed.

"What, pipsqueak?" Jake shouted back.

Jeremy held the broken arms of his Transformer up to where they used to be attached and threw them back down angrily.

"Is the reason you suck because..." Henry was speaking slowly and clearly, as if he were reading a cue card he couldn't quite see comfortably. "Because you wiped," he paused slightly before saying the next word, "shit... into your kitty?" Henry looked to the maple tree.

Jeremy swore he could hear faint whispers but it could also be the wind. Henry continued.

"I mean, your pussy. Do you suck because you wiped shit into your pussy again?" Henry thought for a moment. "Or is it because your mom took away your favorite..." he paused and looked at the tree again, "dildo? Or is it because your mom took away your favorite dildo and the broom handle gives you ass-splinters?"

Jake's eyes were as big as saucers. His lips were sucked in so tight against his teeth it made his whole reddening face quiver. The other nearby students who witnessed this dropped everything they were doing. It was as if someone paused the whole scene, until Jake roared and broke into a run straight for Henry.

Henry wasn't quite sure what was supposed to happen next, and wasn't really sure he particularly cared for ghost games. Jake was in a full sprint now just yards away from Henry. He was fully intending to take this kid the fuck out. As he was just ten feet away from the small ginger boy, he pulled his fist back. He could already see it connecting with the boy's smart mouth.

Bam!

It was not the sound of Jake's fist hitting Henry. It was the sound of Jake's own face colliding with something and it was he who was taken the fuck out! The object that had blocked him from dropping a beat down on Henry seemed to be pushing the blood and spit from his mouth.

Jake was on his back almost immediately. His vision was blurred and there were tiny, bright pops in front of his eyes. He gasped for breath. He could see Henry standing over him looking down, now with his finger in his nose. There was a pain pulsating where his face had made the connection with this object, which he could see now was not floating in midair. It was a fist. A fist in a leather glove, now extending its middle finger, which was attached to an arm.

Behind Henry staring down at Jake appeared two giants, dressed in black with classy hats on. Jake instinctively got back on his feet, slower than he would have preferred. He jumped as he heard a deep, scratchy voice.

"Jake Mortinburg!" Wes was doing his best impression of Christian Bale's version of the Batman.

"W... what?" Jake said in a shaky voice before regaining some nerve. "Who are you guys?"

"You can see them too?!" Henry asked Jake, shocked.

"We're here to give you a message," Wes said in his deep, scratchy voice. "You are going to stop picking on other kids. Tell your friends. It's done."

Jake looked at his own reflection in Wes's sunglasses. The sight of his bloody lip made him angry.

"You're not the boss of me!" He said to Wes, the way only a shitty little kid can truly say that and mean it. Eugene kicked Jake in the ribs, and Jake once again fell to the ground.

"We are so, Jake." Eugene told him factually.

"You are going to play nice from now on, Jake," Wes told him.

"Or what?! I'm going to tell the principal and you're going to get raped in prison!" Jake shouted from the ground.

"You." Wes was getting pretty good at sounding scary. "Will. Tell. *No one.* Now get the fuck up." Jake got the fuck up and immediately got in Wes's face.

"You guys can't just mess with me. I own this playground!"

Jake looked toward the slide. A brown-haired girl who looked to be about eight was climbing up the ladder.

"Sally!" Jake shouted. The girl turned her head toward Jake just as she started to slide down. "Get off my slide!" Though she was only about a third down the slide, she pushed herself over the edge and fell straight down onto her front.

"Besides," he said looking back to Wes and Eugene, "my gang will find you and hunt you down."

"I'm sorry, your gang?" Wes broke his Batman impression. "You mean your other little eleven-year-old friends who don't know any better than to eat their own snot?"

A dozen-or-so other fifth graders approached Jake. The rest of the playground formed a circle around the scene at a safe distance.

"They call us," Jake started, "The Snakes!"

"First of all," a bemused Eugene said to Jake, "No one has *ever* called any of you The Snakes. And secondly," he thought for a bit, "you all need to fuck right off!"

"This is your warning," Wes was once again speaking in an uncomfortably low and scratchy voice. "Stop picking on other kids. Stop hurting them, stealing from them, breaking their toys and otherwise terrorizing them. Or we are going to hurt you very very badly. Do you understand? Is that a deal?"

None of The Snakes took their eyes off Wes and Eugene. It seemed everyone on the playground was waiting for an answer. Except teachers; there were none of those around, which was weird. Jake finally answered.

"No. No deal." He put his fist in the air and shouted as loud as he could, "*Snake bite!*"

All thirteen of The Snakes charged at Wes and Eugene. Henry sloppily ran to get out of the way. Ghost games were confusing. As the gang approached, the two grown men started taking them down. Some were stopped with swift kicks to the head, some with punches to the stomach, and Eugene even managed to slap one or two across the face. One kid grabbed Wes's throat as he was punching another kid. Wes grabbed the hand and used it to slap its owner's face repeatedly. He was finding it very easy to fight eleven-year-olds. Eugene let out a scream as he was bit in the calf.

"Fuck my cock!" he shouted as he grabbed the kid by the hair and pulled their faces close enough to bite him back.

He watched the blood spray out of one kids nose after it collided with the head of the kid Eugene shoved into said nose. Wes grabbed Jake by the collar and shoved his knee into Jake's belly button. He fell to the ground. Some of the kids they'd taken down were getting back up. *That doesn't happen in movies*, Eugene thought to himself. But this wasn't a movie. If it was a movie, it would be a very good movie. But it wasn't a movie. As Wes back-handed a kid across the cheek while stomping on another kid's foot, he heard a buzz and shriek come from next to him. To his surprise, he saw a boy writhing on the ground and a taser in Eugene's hand.

"Dude!" Wes shouted to his sidekick amidst the chaos. "Did you just tase that kid?!"

"Fuck yes I did," Eugene yelled as he kicked a boy in the jaw. "That little son of a bitch was going for my sorry-sack! Now he's sucking a fat, fifteen-thousand-volt dick!"

Wes punched a kid in the face, smearing another kid's blood on the victim in the process.

"Where did you even get a taser?" Wes shouted.

"From the taser store! Why do you keep asking me shit like that?" Again, Wes said nothing back but just kept beating children.

"Why? Are tasers not allowed?" Eugene asked.

"Of course not!" Wes affirmed.

"I got one for you too, buddy!" Eugene pulled another out of his pocket and tossed it to Wes, who caught it and examined it while kicking a kid.

Wes eyed the device and frowned. He pulled the trigger and an electric current was produced on the front. He looked at an angry boy with a bruised and bloodied face running toward him, who'd already been taken down twice. Wes looked at his new toy and then back at the kid and then back at the taser.

Buzz!

The kid fell down, twitching slightly. Wes grinned. He and Eugene started zapping kids left and right until all thirteen were laying awkwardly positioned on the ground, twitching and moaning in pools of blood, spit and probably urine. There was silence. Wes wondered what the next step was. He hadn't thought this far ahead. Frankly, he hadn't intended to do more than punch Jake Mortinburg one time in the face. His concentration was broken by the sudden uproar of applause coming from the students who'd circled to watch The Snakes get obliterated.

"So," Eugene turned to Wes. "Should we go to work now?"

"We should get the fuck out of Dodge," Wes replied. They adjusted their suits and gracelessly sprinted away from the playground.

"There go the two best ghosts in the world," Henry said to another boy his age.

"They were ghosts?" the boy asked, shocked.

"They sure were. And they were my best friends." Henry put his finger back in his nose, pulled it out and examined it. He then wiped it on the jacket of the other boy. The group of students dispersed leaving The Snakes lying on the ground alone as the bell rang.

Wes and Eugene ran to where they had parked Eugene's car, a block away in the other way than the Speedway station, if that matters. Without saying a word, they got in as quickly as they could with Eugene behind the wheel. He started the car and put it in drive and the vehicle lurched forward with a skid into traffic.

The two men started ripping off their hats and masks and capes and jackets as they drove and throwing them into the back seat. When they were about a mile away from the scene, they finally made eye contact with each other, which enticed a giggling fit between them. Wes spoke first.

"Dude."

"Honestly," Eugene said through his laughter, "I had no idea how easy it would be to punch a child."

"I know, right?" Wes agreed. He thought a moment about this. "Does that make us bad people?" He asked Eugene.

"No!" Eugene affirmed. "Being lazy, apathetic, drunk-driving racists make us bad people."

Wes started to laugh but that feeling stopped as he thought about what Eugene just said.

"Wait. I'm not a racist," Wes informed Eugene.

"Oh, I just meant," Eugene seemed to be surprised at his own words. "Bad example." Wes looked at him. "Bad example," he repeated slower without meeting Wes's eyes.

"Are you racist, Eugene?" Wes asked. Eugene answered quickly.

"No! Of course not," he affirmed. "Don't be an idiot! Eat a bunch of dicks!"

"There's no need to be defensive if you have nothing to defend," Wes snarkily stated. They both watched the road roll under them.

"We totally just beat up some kids," Wes finally said out loud.

"I know, I can't stop thinking about it either! Eugene said excitedly. "Did you see this one little bastard bite me?"

"He bit you?!"

"Yeah. In the leg. There's probably a bruise," Eugene speculated.

"Boy, if a kid would have bit me, I'd have--"

"Bit him back? Because that's totally what I did! Right in the face! After I bashed the top of his head." Eugene sounded prouder than he probably should have been.

"You bit a kid's face?" Wes asked surprised. Eugene's only reply was a resurgence of laughter.

"You are one fucked up racist mother fucker." Eugene's laughter stopped. "Probably a black kid," Wes said under his breath but loud enough to be clearly heard.

"Oh fuck off with that shit!" Eugene was hung-over and annoyed. Something suddenly occurred to Wes.

"Hey, what reason did you end up giving our boss for our tardiness?" Wes asked curiously.

"Reason?" Eugene asked confusedly.

"Yes, what did you tell the boss to cover us being late? He wants me dead as it is."

"Oh I just told him we had to beat up some fifth-graders at school and he was cool with it," Eugene sarcastically replied.

"Shut up, what did you really tell him?" Wes was beginning to get nervous.

"Dude, I didn't tell him anything." These words hit Wes in the face like a tiny eleven-year-old fist.

"I thought you were calling in!" he started to yell at Eugene. "I'm not supposed to be late again!"

"Well why on earth couldn't you have called in?" Eugene asked calmly.

"Because," Wes said not calmly, "the boss always gives me shit!"

"Oh I'm sorry. I thought you finally grew a pair," Eugene stated.

"Pair not grown," Wes said worried.

"Well don't worry," Eugene reassured, "I just remembered I have a plan anyway."

Eugene suddenly and violently jerked the wheel to the right. The car immediately skidded off the road with smoke emanating from the tires. Wes grabbed the handle of his door and braced himself, not having any time to think or speak. In an instant, the car was stopped by a utility pole.

The windshield was cracked and broken, the hood was wrapped around the pole, smoke was now coming from under the hood and the passengers' side hubcap toppled to the sidewalk under them. The only sound was the coming from the hub-cap as it lazily spun on edge for a full ten seconds before toppling over on its face.

Wes and Eugene sat motionless, Wes still braced, Eugene's hands still on the wheel and a foolish grin on his mug. After what figuratively felt like an hour, Wes finally had the nerve to speak.

"What?" he finally managed to get out. "*What*?!" He repeated desperately. "What in the world was that?!"

"That," Eugene said smartly, "was me giving us a reason to be late."

"*You did that on purpose?!*" Wes was shocked.

"We are going to be more late," Eugene said matter-of-factly. "Should we get lunch?"

Wes was still in shock. He opened the door and got out of the wreckage. He paced frantically along the car trying to assess the damage. Eugene shouted to him from inside the car.

"You're not hungry?"

Wes climbed back into the passenger seat, now visibly angry.

"Yes, I am hungry," Wes's voice was low and clear. "But unfortunately we have to call the police." Wes was slightly dumbfounded. "And I should probably point out, too, that even though we were just involved in this unfortunate accident, it took place over an hour after we were supposed to be at work. How are you going to explain that?" Eugene blinked.

"I don't think anybody's going to ask," he finally determined. "And we're certainly not going to call the police with all this evidence in the car."

"Evidence?" Wes asked without thinking.

"You know, our sweet costumes that I'm sure are covered with tons and tons of DNA?"

"Shit," Wes realized he was exactly right. "Well, let's ditch all that shit someplace and call a tow truck." Just as Wes said that they both noticed the illumination of red and blue lights blinking in the rear-view mirror growing larger and larger.

"Well, there's probably no time for that," Eugene pointed out as the police car came to an abrupt stop behind them.

They immediately started pulling off the elements of their costumes they were still wearing and shoving them in the back seat. Wes managed to push everything under the capes on top. "That looks exactly like we're hiding a body under there," Eugene said just as the police officer approached his window.

"Is anybody hurt?" the cop asked cautiously. Wes and Eugene were now sitting there looking straight ahead, each wearing short-sleeved white dress shirts, black ties, and black dress pants.

"No sir," Wes replied as guilt-free as possible.

"You mind telling me why you've parked your vehicle around this utility pole?" the officer asked without a hint of sympathy or concern in his voice. Eugene caught a glimpse of Wes and himself in the rear-view mirror and was hit with inspiration.

"We're Mormons," he told the officer. As the officer opened his mouth in disbelief, Wes preempted his thought before any words could come out.

"What he means is--" Wes looked the police man directly in the face for the first time and recognized the man he saw. He was instantly filled with surprise, doubt and dread all at once. These emotions pushed his next sentence out of his mouth.

"Holy fuck, Evan Thomas?"

"Yes?" the officer said as he lifted his sun-glasses and took a good look at the men in the car. He was tall and muscular and had the same dumb looking face they remembered from school. Evan began to recognize them.

"Aww shit, you've got to be fucking kidding me."

"Hi, Evan," Eugene said as flatly as he could. Evan spat on the ground.

"I don't know why I'm surprised a couple of retards like you crashed your car. Let me guess. You got up extra early to get drunk and have sex with each other and then went for a romantic drive, right into this pole? It's adorable, really. You two will fit right in, in prison." Evan's voice told them this was not going to go well.

"We are not drunk or gay *and you know that, Evan!*" The words came instinctively out of Wes's mouth before he could really stop them.

"Really though dipshits. Why did you crash your car?"

"Because we were late for work," Eugene told him honestly.

"What he means is he crashed the car and now we're late for work," Wes corrected. "And the reason we crashed is because..." Wes hesitated and looked at Eugene.

"He was giving me road head. His big, beautiful mouth was right around my hard shaft." Eugene's explanation did not please anyone. Evan processed what Eugene just told him before speaking again.

"I fucking hate you guys. But that does explain the god damn capes in your back seats. And the bite marks."

"We're not..." Wes couldn't find his words. "A dog ran out in the road and Eugene lost control of the car trying to avoid killing the thing."

"It was a wiener dog in the road. Except without the *dog* and by 'road' he means his--"

"Do you really think you're helping?!" Wes shouted at Eugene. Evan continued to look at them with his dumb, stupid homophobic face.

"Well, I'm putting both stories in my report, but I know what I believe. Something is really weird about this. I'll be in my car until the tow truck gets here. Stay in your car, don't bother me, and don't blow each other."

They watched Evan walk back to his car. Once he was in the law enforcement vehicle and out of sight, Wes slapped Eugene square in the face.

"How could you possibly have thought saying that shit was a good idea?" Wes asked Eugene, who was rubbing his cheek.

"Dude's an asshole homophobe! Fuck that shit! If he's that dumb I want to do everything I can to make him uncomfortable," Eugene replied with fire in his eyes.

"Pretty passionate coming from a racist," Wes said.

CHAPTER 4: Hardly Workin'

The office plaza where Wes and Eugene worked was buzzing with white noise. Wes had often thought that it was the only place on Earth where silence could be so loud. It was a steady mixture of typing, phones ringing, fan-blades spinning and indiscriminate talking of about a hundred people.

Telescom was the third-biggest telemarketing company based in Wes's hometown, out of the three it had. Anyone who walked through the public entrance was greeted by a reception desk, which is where Lance McGrott was headed looking in a right pissed mood. Behind the desk sat a woman who was gross.

Joan was a fat woman in her early 40s who was never taught how to dress herself appropriately. Her clothes were too tight and too revealing and her makeup seemed to contain every color contained within the spectrum of visible light. Her hair had been bleached blonde so often that it lost the properties of normal human hair and behaved more like a curly bundle of twigs. Lance was never happy to have to talk to her because she was gross.

"Joan, have you heard anything from Wes or Eugene?" Lance asked her carefully looking right into her eyes and not letting them drift lower, which is where she would have preferred his eyes to go.

"No sir," she said, trying her best to sound like a lady and not like a sloppy, gross mess. "I have not."

"It's almost noon. They're both three hours late."

"Would you like me to try to call them, Sir?" she asked.

"No," Lance replied. "This will give me a reason to make the rest of their day a living hell."

"You make my day special, Sir," she said grossly. "If you need me to do anything, please let me know." She shifted her terrible body so more of her fat, veiny breasts slopped out from behind her already straining blouse.

"Anything."

"You know what I'd really like you to do, Joan?"

Lance leaned in and lowered his voice. Joan's face flushed slightly from under the pound of makeup she caked onto her joules.

"What?" she quivered. Lance inched his face nearer, his voice even lower.

"What I'd really like you to do..."

"Yes?" she panted.

Lance's face was now an inch from hers, his voice now a whisper. She could feel his coffee-breath tickling her like the worst feathers ever made.

"Don't eat so much food," he breathed.

He let that sink in before backing the fuck off and going back the way he came.

"Yeah," Joan said to herself. "Give it to me straight," she said biting her lip.

As her mind wandered to places nobody possibly wants to know about, her daydream was broken by Wes and Eugene trying to hurry past the desk without having to stop. It was no use as Joan beckoned them

"Guys, get over here." The two visibly disheveled men stopped in their tracks, looked up at the ceiling and sighed heavily, turned around and started toward the reception desk.

"What, Joan?" Eugene asked impatiently.

"Your best friend was just asking about you two," she told them.

"Well, I crashed my car. I don't even know why we came here. We need to go home. I think I have whiplash. But I'm sorry if our trauma has inconvenienced you in any way," Eugene angrily told her to try and stop the conversation.

Wes stood and nodded silently. Joan gasped, placing her right hand over her heart, which while it was there, she gave herself a couple of tender tweaks.

"Oh, you poor, poor things! Do you two need Mommy to comfort you?" Joan was gross. "Both of you? At the same time?" Wes and Eugene shuddered. "Mommy can make both of you feel so good."

"Can you please not sexually harass us this afternoon? It's kind of been a hard day already," Wes said. He had never had much of a problem saying what needed to be said.

"Mmm. That's what I like to hear." Joan stuck a pencil in her mouth and chewed "seductively."

"I'm going to my cube now," Wes said.

"Me too," Eugene followed.

The two walked away toward their cubicles, both frowning. Joan pulled the pencil from her mouth and put it back down the front of her shirt. Eugene came to his cube first and wordlessly went to his desk. Wes walked a few more feet and entered his own workspace, immediately seeing someone sitting in his spot. The chair turned slowly and dramatically around to face him.

"So Wes," Lance started, "is it tardy out today? Maybe just retardy."

"Look, Eugene and I were in a car accident this morning. I don't even know if I can work the rest of the day," Wes explained.

"Wes, you have too many important calls to make to be taking days off. How will people know how much they can save by switching to us for long distance if we don't call them at home and tell them?"

"First of all, I don't even know anyone who has a land-line anymore. These calls haven't been relevant since stand-up comedy in the nineties. And secondly, my shit is still all fucked up from you throwing it on the ground."

Wes gestured to everything he needed to do his job being in a pile on the floor except for his keyboard and mouse, which someone put back on the desk.

"And this whole cubicle block still smells like piss."

"You know what else it smells like, Wes?" Wes blinked. "Failure."

"I'm pretty sure those two smells are very similar," Wes told his unamused boss.

"Don't talk back to me right now," Lance said to Wes. "If you value your job, you will do what you're told. And right now, I'm telling you to make some calls. And also, that you're a fat, dumb idiot and I wish you would have died in that car accident, just so I could defecate in your coffin before it's in the ground."

Lance started to take his graceful exit from the cubicle before turning around to add, "Defecate means poop!" He was gone.

Wes sat down in his chair that was still warm from the heat of Lance's body. Out of everything, this made Wes feel the most uncomfortable. He was defeated. All of the feelings of vigilante justice from standing up for the little guy were washed clean out of his heart and replaced with the usual bleak emptiness.

He took a deep breath and bent down to the pile of his work things, picked up the computer and placed it on his desk. Noticing that all the cords were still attached and plugged in, he pressed the power button. The happy sound of Windows 98 loading greeting him. Wes absent-mindedly did the math to figure out just how old that software was.

He bent down and retrieved his phone and headset, which had come unplugged from his cubicle phone jack. He put the headset on, plugged it into the receiver, and attached the phone to the line completing the connection. Within two seconds, his phone rang and Wes jumped slightly with surprise.

He blinked. The phone rang a second time. He usually just made outgoing calls from this phone. He pressed a button on his headset and answered suspiciously.

"Hello?"

"Wesly, I've been--"

"Thank you for calling Telescom," he interrupted the woman's voice. "How may I--"

"*God dammit* I've been trying to call you all morning! How come you didn't answer your cell phone?" Bonnie asked in a panic.

"Because I'm at work," Wes told her, failing completely to not sound suspicious.

"You've been there all day?" Wes thought for a moment before answering Bonnie's question.

"Yes," he finally decided to say.

"Then why didn't you answer any of my calls?"

"What do you think this is? You called and I answered!"

"But you didn't answer any of the dozen times I called before! Why?" Bonnie was furious.

"Well," Wes paused to think. "Because. Because of some secrets."

There was silence on the other end of the phone. Wes was hoping this would catch Bonnie off guard enough for her to drop it and get to why she was calling him in the first place. His plan seemed to work.

"That's a weird thing to say," she finally answered. "Whatever. But get this! Jeremy e-mailed me from school earlier telling me that two crazy men beat up another kid and his gang at school today!"

"Oh, what?" Wes was unintentionally overplaying his reaction. Someone who wasn't in the middle of sharing breaking news might have noticed how unconvincing he sounded.

"Yeah, two grown men!" Bonnie went on.

"Wow, that's super crazy and unexpected!" Wes still sounded like he was forcing unnatural words out of his mouth hole. "Did you hear any details? Like, does anyone know who they are or why or anything at all incriminating about them? Did anyone say they were ruggedly handsome?"

"No, but it was that kid Jake who's been picking on all of the other kids, including Jeremy."

"Oh. Well, that's pretty awesome," Wes told her reassuringly.

"Awesome? *Awesome?!*" Wes had to pull his headset away from his face to avoid damaging his eardrum. "It's not awesome! My child could have been seriously hurt!" Bonnie shouted.

"Your child? I thought the bully got beat up. That means Jeremy is safe, right? No more bruises?"

"Today, it was that shitty bully kid. Tomorrow, who knows?"

It was starting to occur to Wes that what he and Eugene had done might be upsetting to others, other than Jake and his gang of bitches.

"You really think they'll strike again, Bonnie?" Wes was curious of her answer, partly because he had not yet considered a repeat of that morning ever being a possibility.

"I just don't know. The school didn't close, which is bullshit, but everyone is weirded out. And they are going to maintain better security on the school grounds."

These words went into Wes's ear the way Joan often thought her tongue might: uninvited.

"What kind of security?" Wes asked, trying to sound the right kind of curious.

"I don't know," Bonnie answered. "Is that really important?"

"Yes," Wes simply said.

"Well, maybe. But, what is more important is that I'm taking Jeremy out of school for the rest of the day. Maybe longer. And I just don't know if I feel safe alone." Wes was starting to feel guilty, which made him feel weird about realizing he had not felt the least bit guilty for terrorizing those bullies.

"Does Gary know yet?"

"I called him first. He just started crying," Bonnie said, not trying to hide the tone in her voice.

"Wesley," Bonnie started. Her voice was different now. It had become softer and higher. "I hate to ask this of you, but is there any way you can get out of work early? I'd feel safer at your apartment. As far as I know they didn't catch those psychos, meaning they could still be out targeting children!"

"Well, Gene and I got in a car accident, so I was--"

"What?!" Wes winced as he again pulled the headset away from his face. "What else can go wrong today?!" she pleaded.

"Probably nothing," he said knowingly. "Hey, Bonnie?"

"What?" Wes chose his words thoughtfully.

"I wouldn't worry too much about those guys. They're probably just... I don't know," he didn't want to sound too sympathetic. "They're probably just doing what they think is right."

These weren't the right words at all.

"What they think is right?" Bonnie's voice was lower and serious. "What the fuck is wrong with you? If I ever meet the men who went to my son's school and beat up kids, I swear to Zeus I will remove their balls from the weird ball-bags your type keeps between your legs."

Wes wasn't sure if Bonnie worded that correctly, but winced at it nonetheless.

"Go get Jeremy," Wes said into his telephone headset. "Be at my apartment in a half hour."

"Thanks Wesley, I owe you!" Bonnie seemed to be cheered up, or at least comforted.

"No worries," he told her. "I'll see you soon. Click."

He pressed the end call button immediately after saying *click*. After last night's phone conversation, he was contemplating making that his new thing.

He sat pondering the situation he and Eugene had created. It wasn't supposed to uproot the whole community. But maybe it's a good thing it did! If this is widely spread around, he and Eugene could have effectively ended bullying! Maybe it'll be on the news! But if it's on the news, then that means it's a news story. And news stories get investigated. That would probably be a problem.

Wes's thinking was interrupted by a chime sounding on his computer. An instant message window popped up on his screen. The message was from someone using the handle *GENIEBOTTLE1980*.

GENIEBOTTLE1980: Dude, Jake Mortinburg is pissed!

Wes typed a response back to Eugene in the reply box and hit enter.

HowTheWESwasWon: ?

GENIEBOTTLE1980: He made a vid... I think 4 us

HowTheWESwasWon: What? How do you know?

GENIEBOTTLE1980: I searched 4 his name on uTube & this was posted 1/2 hr ago:

Wes's computer chimed again as *GENIEBOTTLE1980* made a hyperlink pop up in the text window. Wes clicked it curiously. His internet browser opened and was directed to YouTube, where a video titled *Jake's Revenge* started to load.

Wes's eyes widened. The video, obviously shot with a smartphone, opened with a shot of the ground clumsily panning up to Jake's slightly out-of-frame face. Jake looked directly into the camera, thus effectively into Wes's eyes as he was the one watching the video, and spoke.

"Nobody. Nobody beats up Jake Mortinburg. Here's why."

The camera shot panned to a line of what appeared to be about ten small children, their ages ranging from kindergarten to third-grade, each restrained and held in place by a different beat-up looking member of The Snakes. It was hard to make out faces due to the quality of the streaming video and shoddy camera work.

Jake walked all the way to the left side of the line and stomped on the small child's foot before punching her in the stomach. He did this to every other kid in the row until they were all wheezing, whimpering or crying. He shot a look of fury into the camera. From out of frame, a voice was heard.

"Worth it!"

Wes recognized Jeremy's voice before the camera panned to reveal who was speaking. Wes's stomach turned inside-out and back again. Jeremy was being held in place at the end of the line by a boy with now visible bite-marks on his cheek.

"I'd take ten punches to the stomach to see you jerks beat up like that again! It was worth it!" The video now showed Jake walking up to Jeremy.

"Have it your way, Germ-y," Jake told him as he brought his fist back.

He counted out loud. Each number was called as his fist connected with Jeremy's abdomen. If Jeremy hadn't been held in place by a goon, he would have been doubled over on the ground. The wind was knocked completely out of him. Jake turned toward the camera and approached it, his face now taking up most of the frame.

"I don't know who you guys were, but I will not be told what to do. I am eleven years old! If you ever show up again, every student in school will get a black eye, compliments of Jake Mortinburg!" His eyes were wild and there was spit foaming at the corers of his mouth. "Do you understand? Is that a deal?" he asked mockingly before the video ended.

Wes recognized those as the final words he'd given to Jake around two and a half hours ago.

"Mother fuck," Wes said to himself. His eyes narrowed and he mouth tensed. "It's on."

A few seconds after saying that, his computer chimed again, alerting an instant message.

GENIEBOTTLE1980: its on!!!!

Wes typed a reply.

HowTheWESwasWon: Did you hear me? I just said that out loud!

GENIEBOTTLE1980: OMG no way! Awesome!

HowTheWESwasWon: Hey let's leave work because of whiplash.

GENIEBOTTLE1980: LOL I already put on my coat

*

Evan Thomas pulled his police car into a parking spot. He was not in a good mood. Evan had not seen or thought about Wes or Eugene in over a decade. His hatred for them was irrational, but it boiled back to the surface nonetheless. How dare they still exist. How dare they be grown up and live in his town! The town that he serves and protects.

Except Evan did not really concern himself that much with serving and protecting. His sole motivation for earning his badge was power and authority. Good police officers are intimidating. Evan was a dick. He stormed into the station, grabbed a donut from a box on someone's desk not meant for him, took a bite as he walked, and immediately threw it toward a garbage can, which he missed. How dare that donut not be full of jelly! Even though it was a traditional round donut with a hole and sprinkles. He pushed open an office door with his fist. It was the office of Detective Wade Wadeler.

Wade and Evan grew up together, teaming up to terrorize anyone they hated, which was everyone. When they were young, Wade was kind of the sidekick. Sometime around middle school, however, something happened to Wade that changed him. Evan never managed to get out of him what it was, but it was implied that he had seen someone get killed. Or maybe it was that he had seen someone get born. Either way, he was never the same.

"Wade, you're not going to believe who I just saw," Evan said to Wade in an angry voice, spitting donut crumbs as he spoke and slamming the office door shut.

"I believe everything you ever say to me," Wade told him. "Until you give me reason to believe nothing."

The words came out of Wade's ever-pissed-off-looking face. He was slightly stocky with short, neat black hair and sideburns. Standing next to the thin Evan who sported a blonde mustache, he looked more like an older brother than sidekick.

"Remember in school there was that fat fucking loser, something Westin? Wes? And we always took his lunch and shit?" Wade leaned back in his chair and put the tips of his fingers together.

"Every day," he said. "Every day I wake up and look at myself in the mirror. Should I shave? Does it matter? Am I where I want to be? Who is this person looking back? Are there things I regret?"

Evan was used to this kind of behavior from Wade, but it didn't make it any less annoying.

"And every time I get to that question, I think of Wes." Wade's eyes closed. "I think of him. And it just makes me sick. The way we treated him? Every day, Evan, we took his lunch. Every. Day."

Evan was starting to worry that this might be guilt.

"But, not once – *not once!* - did we take his money or his bike." Wade slammed his fist down on his desk, "*and it makes me sick!*"

"So yes? You do remember?" Evan finally asked.

"More than I remember anything else in the world," Wade said with a vacant stare in his eyes.

"That's weird. But hey, he was still hanging out with his butt-buddy Eugene," Evan said.

"Wait." Wade thought. "They grew up together and still hang out with each other?"

"Yeah and from what they said, it sounds like they work together too," Evan told him.

"Losers of that caliber make me *sick*," Wade said with a laugh. Evan joined in laughing too, both of them failing to recognize the irony of their laughter.

"So anyway, those two cock-mouths crashed their car today," Evan said, still chuckling.

"Oh good. Are they dead?" Wade asked, not at all kidding.

"Unfortunately not."

"Did you bring them in? You could have Weird Pete give them his 'all inclusive' strip search," Wade suggested.

"Dammit, I didn't think of that," Evan said realizing the missed opportunity. "But I did have their car impounded. It's getting towed to Lomez's right now." Wade's face cracked with a hint of smile.

"Lomez is still following your special instructions, I presume?"

"That's what I pay him for! Piece of shit car will be stripped and shipped by next week. Hope I don't screw up any paperwork when it's undoubtedly reported," Evan said, his eyes alive with mischief.

"Good. And speaking of payoffs," Wade said through what was now a full grin, "I just received a nice chunk of change for 'not finding any prints' at the Bertagnoli house."

He produced a small paper bag with the top rolled-shut from inside his trench coat. Wade wasn't the kind of guy to take off his trench coat just because he was inside. Or ever. He tossed the bag to Evan who shoved it down the front of his pants and then gestured to the bulge in his crotch.

"Awesome. I bet you didn't find the missing gun, either?" Evan said with a glint in his eye.

"I sure didn't. I also didn't scratch the serial number off of it and sell it on the corner to an Arab man. For cheap. Also, there's glint in your eye."

"Oh thanks," Evan said as he wiped away the glint. "You know, there was something about seeing those two today."

Evan seemed to be deep in thought as he said this, which was an unusual state for him.

"Something that makes me want to pee on something of theirs."

"I'm surprised you didn't plant any coke on them. They'd have been fucked for life," Wade said.

"I didn't want to waste any of my coke."

Wade power-high-fived Evan. Evan started rummaging through the office.

"I'm surprised we haven't crossed paths since school. I ran both of their licenses. Clean. How could these two fuck-ups not have anything so much as a speeding ticket?"

Evan finished speaking as he retrieved what he must have been looking for: a big, brown briefcase. He pulled a key out of his pocket.

"I'd wager that maybe there was one set of footprints in the sand, as it were." Wade sometimes turned to quoting scripture.

Evan nodded as he unlocked the briefcase and flipped it open as Wade continued.

"When you've been through what I have, you know that there is someone with you, always. And he is vengeful."

Evan pulled a zip-top bag out of the aluminum-foil-lined briefcase. It was packed full of white powder. He tossed it to Wade.

"Want to snort this out of our guns?" Evan asked.

"Yes," Wade answered.

*

Wes and Eugene were sitting on the couch at Wes's apartment waiting for Bonnie. By this time, the gravity of their situation had completely sunk in. Wes was starting to think that maybe they hadn't thought everything completely through before resorting to brutal violence. Eugene was pretty sure they did the right thing, regardless of consequences.

"Jake Mortinburg is a piece of shit," Eugene said out of the blue.

"We are going to need to plan our next attack," Wes said staring forward.

"Yeah. He can't get away with that video. Snotty little fuck."

"Do you think maybe we've just made things worse?" Wes sounded worried, because he was.

"Wes," Eugene sighed. "Do you know anything about getting water in melting chocolate?"

"Why the fuck would you be melting chocolate?"

"For chocolate fondue or something," Eugene said defensively.

"You have a lot of fondue parties I don't know about, Gene?"

"Maybe!" Eugene had never had a fondue party. "Point is, if you're melting chocolate on the stove and you drip water in it, it will seize up and get all weird."

"Oh, what a tragic, fucking end to the fondue party." Wes was in no mood for bullshit. "Do you remember what has gone on today?"

"Listen. The only way to fix it is to keep adding more and more water. Maybe getting water in the chocolate was a mistake. But it can be fixed with more water and proper technique." Wes thought about what Eugene was saying.

"Water was the problem and the solution?"

"Yes!" Eugene replied.

"So, we can still dip our sliced strawberries and Oreos in the fondue?" Wes said mockingly.

"Are you getting my point at all?" Eugene asked becoming irritated.

"Do you ever just wake up thinking 'Oh my god, this is a chocolate day?' I crave chocolate when I'm menstruating too, Eugene."

Eugene calmed himself and spoke in a low and steady voice, as though he was trying to reason with a toddler.

"I'm saying that even if we made it worse, the only way to make it better is with more beat downs. Until this little pecker-face learns."

"'Little pecker-face,'" Wes repeated, "As in, it's a small pecker that he has for a face, or he's little and also is a pecker-face, but it may or may not be a normal sized pecker?"

"Obviously, the second one. Do you get anything I'm saying?" Eugene was afraid to even ask.

"Well yeah. I'm not a fucking idiot," Wes replied. "I was just confused about your weird fantasy of having to save the fancy fondue party."

Eugene turned away from Wes and a small black cloud seemed to figuratively rise from the top of his head.

Eugene's annoyance was interrupted by a knock on the door. Before either of them could stand, the door swung open and Jeremy bolted inside, clutching an action figure and making it fight with other objects in the room. Bonnie followed, her face red and puffy. She had been crying but was trying to put on a cool demeanor.

Wes greeted her with a hug. She grabbed him and pulled him in tightly, burying her face in his shoulder. After a moment, her head lifted and her grasp loosened. She looked Wes in the face, her eyes pleading for comfort. Wes always had a hard time keeping inappropriate grins at bay and a twinge of glee surfaced at the corners of his mouth. Bonnie didn't seem to notice as she let go of him and started toward the couch.

Eugene raised his arms to gesture for a hug but Bonnie walked past. Eugene put his arms down, hoping no one noticed his rejected hug, which Wes did. The three sat down in their usual positions on Wes's old couch. Jeremy was now making his toy fight DVD cases near Wes's television.

"Guys," Bonnie said as her voice quivered, "I'm so sorry for making you leave work early. I just..." her nostrils flared as she gathered breath to speak. "I just didn't want to be alone right now."

"Seriously, never apologize for supplying us with a reason to ditch the office," Wes reassured her. He looked at Jeremy, who had broken the case for a DVD copy of *Back to the Future II* and was now trying to put it back together.

"Jeremy, don't worry about that, it's Eugene's copy anyway. Are you okay? Do you want to talk about what happened at school?" Jeremy's face lit up.

"Of course I do! I was *awesome!*" he screamed, smashing his toy onto Wes's carpeted floor and adding what he must have perceived as karate sound-effects. "These two men showed up and kicked the poop out of Jake Mortinburg and his butt friends!"

"I heard about that, Jake," Wes told him. "But did anything else happen to you? Did you get picked on or beat up?"

"Like were you part of a weird elementary school cellphone snuff film today?" Eugene asked before getting a look from Wes. Eugene shrugged. Jeremy's smile shined.

"Today was great!" he said, as he went running into the kitchen undoubtedly looking for other things for his toy to fight and break.

"I just don't know what to do with him," Bonnie sighed. "I can't take him back to that school. Who knows when those monsters will come back and target other students!"

"'Monsters' seems a little harsh..." Eugene muttered under his breath.

"Bonnie, I promise, everything will be fine." Wes did his best to sound reassuring and not suspicious. "Maybe just let him stay home sick tomorrow." Bonnie didn't seem to like these words.

"And then what, Wes?" she asked accusingly. "He takes a day off from school. Then what?"

"And then nut the fuck up and take him back!" Eugene said authoritatively. "Come on. No one was seriously hurt. If anything, the school will now be safer!"

Bonnie looked at Eugene as though she were looking at a brick floating in the sky. Her eyes narrowed in disbelief.

"How the hell does this make the school safer, Gene?"

"Jeremy was getting beat up. Another kid got beat up by some dudes. This might actually get the attention of the people in charge at school to make sure kids are safe on the playground. You think the police - let alone the administrators of the school! - would allow something like this to happen again? Not fucking--" as Eugene realized what he was saying, his eyes met Wes's who must have realized the same thing. They shared the same worried look. Eugene's voice calmed, "likely," he finished.

Jeremy came tearing into the room with his toy in one hand and the handle of a coffee mug in his other. There was no sign of the rest of the mug.

"Maybe you have a point," Bonnie said to Eugene. "I don't know. All I want to do is curl up with my son and watch cartoons." Jeremy jumped into her lap and gave her a big hug, accidentally jamming the coffee mug-handle into her spine.

"Good idea," Wes stated. "Jeremy, pick out a movie."

He got back off the couch, handing Wes the mug handle as he headed toward the DVD collection. Wes instinctively poked Eugene in the face with it for no reason.

The apartment was basked in the comforting familiar blue glow of television. There were two empty pizza boxes on the floor next to seven empty cans of Pabst Blue Ribbon. Squeezed onto the couch were Eugene, Bonnie, Jeremy and Wes, Jeremy half in between his mom and Wes, half on top of them.

The only two dry eyes on the couch belonged to the youngest one there. Wes, holding the remote control in his hand, turned down the music playing over the credits that were scrolling along the screen.

"I'm so glad the rat got to open his own kitchen," Wes said doing his best to pretend that his voice wasn't an inch from cracking.

"He will no longer withstand the oppression for being a rat that likes to cook. His only crime: rendering his food too delicious," Eugene added.

"Rats are disgusting. I don't know who would make a kids' movie about rodents in a kitchen with food. He probably got rabies in everything he made!" Bonnie said. Typical.

"You," Wes wiped a tear from his eye. "You just don't get it!"

"Can we watch it again?" Jeremy asked hopefully.

"No, Buddy. We should get going," Bonnie answered before turning to Wes. "Thanks for letting us stay here for the

103

afternoon. And Eugene," She turned and made eye contact with that other guy. "Thanks for..." she tried to find words, "never ever having anything at all better to do than whatever Wes is doing."

"Why screw with the system?" Eugene replied.

Jeremy gave both men high-fives before taking his mom's hand. Wes watched as they walked out and shut the door behind them.

"I don't know why you two don't get fucking married," Eugene said. His statement was greeted with a punch in the shoulder.

"I think we may have severely underestimated the possible consequences of our actions," Wes told Eugene, who was now rubbing his shoulder. Eugene could tell what Wes was considering and didn't like it.

"Dude, you saw the video. If we give up, he wins. And if he wins, Jeremy loses. And if Jeremy loses..." Eugene eyed Wes up and down. He wasn't sure how to put his next statement. "then he ends up a pathetic, fat slob who doesn't even have the scrote to tell a girl he's loved his whole life how he feels about her."

"Subtle," Wes said expressionless.

"I only put it that way because you are a pathetic, fat slob who doesn't even have the scrote to tell a girl he's loved his whole life how he feels about her."

"No, I get it," Wes said, this time a hint of fire in his voice. "But both of our cars are impounded."

"So, we take a cab for a while longer," Eugene replied.

"I'm going to start with the most obvious things wrong with your statement. If a cab driver drops us off at a school, he will be suspicious. Maybe not 'Hey, I bet those two ass-clowns are about to rain thunder on a couple of fifth-graders suspicious, but suspicious nonetheless. Also, where is your costume?"

"In my back seat." As soon as the words left his mouth, Eugene realized this was an additional problem. "Oh."

"Do you have any money to get your car back?" Wes asked, knowing the answer.

"Nope. I'm gonna go ahead and guess you also do not have any money."

"Correct." As Wes answered, Eugene looked hopeless.

"So what you're telling me is--" Eugene started, but his thought was never finished as Wes completed his statement for him.

"That we need to get drunk, break into the impound lot, and get our stuff. And maybe cars as well?" Eugene lit up at Wes's brilliance.

"I thought that might be it. I'll get the gin."

"Yeah, get the gin, Gene." Wes thought about what he'd just said. "Gin, Gene. Gene, gin." He repeated those words for the next several minutes until he was struck in the head by the bottle cap which was thrown at him by Eugene.

CHAPTER 5: Alive!

It wasn't particularly warm for being a night in May, but it wasn't that cold either. On the edge of town, there was a quiet lot of cars surrounded on all sides by chain-link fence, probably about eight feet high. There were tall light-poles every few yards casting patches of illumination and scattered shadows. Two men approached the fence on uneasy feet.

"Have you ever climbed a fence before?" Wes asked Eugene.

"Of course, when I was escaping The Rock," Eugene sarcastically replied.

"Dwayne Johnson kidnapped you?" Wes retorted.

"That's not funny! You know I was referencing that movie about Alcatraz with--"

"Just get the fuck over the fence!"

Eugene approached the chain-link wall and looked directly up. It didn't seem that tall. This was going to be easy. He stepped back a few feet, took a running start, and jumped at the fence grabbing hold of it like a naughty cat latches itself to a screen door. Get down, you naughty cat! After a few seconds of deciding where to go from here, Eugene's grip failed him and he fell flat down onto his back. Wes walked over and loomed above.

"That was not a good way to scale a fence," he said flatly. "Possibly not the worst way. I think getting a shovel and digging under would have been a worse way to climb a fence, but your way was not good."

"Fucking," Eugene started a lot of sentences this way when he needed to make sure the recipient of his words knew he was mad, but wasn't quite sure yet what to say. "Let's see how you climb a fence, tugboat!"

"Tugboat? That's new. And I will climb the fence. I sure as fuck won't need to use my spider-senses to do it."

Wes heard Eugene call him a nerd as he stood face-to-face with the fence. Face-to-fence. He climbed up a few feet, but lost his footing and jumped down. Eugene stood back up and Wes turned to him.

"Maybe if I push you," he suggested to Eugene.

At that instant, Eugene shoved Wes in the chest causing him to stumble backward a couple of steps.

"What the fuck, dude?!" Wes shouted.

"You said you were going to push me! Well, what's up now, bro? I pushed you back!"

"It's not pushing back until I push you first," Wes explained. "And I meant over the fucking fence, you dumb dick." Eugene blinked.

"Right. That was my fault. Okay, almost ready."

Eugene produced a small, silver flask from the inside pocket of his coat. He unscrewed the cap and took a sip before offering it to Wes. Wes obliged and took a heavy pull before passing it back. Eugene put the flask back in his coat as he got in the ready position.

Wes crouched behind him with his hands locked together forming a crude step, where Eugene placed his dirty black Converse sneaker. Wes pushed up on the shoe as Eugene pulled himself up to almost the top. Once he was close enough, he noticed something on top of the fence. There was angry, twisty, pointy hurty wire looping all along the metal wall.

"There's barbed wire up here!" He whisper-shouted to Wes, who was right under him.

"Don't touch it. That shit will give you tetanus," Wes pointed out using a similar loud-whisper.

"Thanks for the advice, Doctor Who."

"Doctor Who isn't a medical doctor with patients and shit, and that's not his name," Wes informed Eugene.

"Then why is that the name of the show?" Eugene asked.

"He goes by 'The Doctor' and sometimes people are like 'Doctor? Doctor Who?' and it's this thing that happens from time to time."

"So then why isn't it called *The Doctor*?" Eugene asked, still whisper-shouting?

"You know, Eugene, you've been asking all sorts of questions about this show for years. Why won't you just watch it with me?" Wes had been telling his friend about this show for a long time.

"It's too intimidating! It's been on for forever and I don't know where to start!"

"I can help you with that," Wes excitedly whispered up to Eugene, who almost seemed to have forgotten he was hanging from a fence. "There are tons of episodes designed to be jumping-on points that fill you in about what the show is. I'll make you a list."

"That would be great," Eugene whispered down to Wes.

"But first you should figure out what to do about this fence," Wes reminded Eugene.

Eugene had forgotten he was hanging from a fence. He turned his head upward and studied the doom ahead of him. Before Wes saw what he was trying to do, Eugene managed to use all of his upper body strength to push off of the highest safe part of the fence and kind of fling himself to the other side, missing the barbed wire completely.

He also missed anywhere to grip onto and fell straight down onto his front. A small cloud of dust upset around his body. He said nothing. Wes said nothing from the other side of the fence. Eugene continued to say nothing. Finally Wes offered words.

"Eugene?" A few moments passed before a weak sound came out of Eugene's mouth, muffled by the dirt.

"Yeah?" he asked.

"Do you think climbing down the wall would have been a better choice than flinging your body to the ground?"

"Yeah," Eugene agreed, weaker than his first reply.

"And can we agree that without the limbering and numbing properties of alcohol you'd probably be dead now?" Wes asked.

"Yeah." Eugene said.

"Can you get up?" Eugene thought about Wes's question before answering.

"It is at this point uncertain."

Wes looked up and down the fence decided how he should go about this. Something caught the corner of his eye. Not something sharp. In fact it wasn't his eye that was caught. It was his attention.

About fifteen feet to the right of them was a large gate, which was open. Wes walked to the gate and looked at it. He blinked. He walked through the gate and back over to Eugene who was still on the ground. He stood above his fallen friend.

"Especially when The Doctor either regenerates or gets a new companion. Or both! They usually use that as an opportunity to re-set the show." Wes explained as he bent down to help Eugene to his feet.

"Did you..." Eugene started to ask.

"No, I didn't," Wes said before he could finish.

He then gestured toward the gate with his head. Eugene stared. What came out of Eugene next could have been mistaken for a sweet dance, but a better description would have been that he was punching and beating up the air in a fury. It stopped after just a few seconds. He composed himself. If this was a movie, there might have been one of those very funny trombone *wah-wah* noises that are so memorably heard in all of the great comedy classics. That sound is very, very funny.

"Alright. Let's go get our goddamned cars back." Eugene said as the two men each darted off to opposite ends of the impound lot.

Just a few yards up a small drive past the gate was a tiny booth, in which sat a small man in a blue suit. In front of this man were several television screens. On one screen, there were rotating shots of different parts of the lot. On another screen, was the local news. On yet another screen was the man's Facebook newsfeed. But on the screen that had held his attention for the past few minutes were two men running away from the outside fence in opposite directions.

The guard, who had just watched the entire debacle, realized he had forgotten to lock the gate again. He was kicking himself because had he remembered to lock the gate, it would probably have been way more entertaining to watch. Now that they were both inside the lot, however, he knew he had to do something about it. The guard always felt kind of bad whenever *their kind* got into the lot. It happened more than one would think. He picked up his hand radio, pressed a button and spoke into it.

"Paul, it's happening again. Two mentally handicapped individuals seem to have gotten away from the home down the road and are playing hide-and-seek in the lot. Why don't you send a cop or something on in and scare 'em up a bit? One of these days one'a'em's gonna get hurt."

"Copy that, a fuzz is on the way," said a voice coming through the tinny radio speaker. The guard pressed the button again.

"You should have seen these two climb my fence, though. Just a hoot!"

In the lot, Wes and Eugene had been up and down several rows of cars and were now within shouting distance of each other.

"I found mine!" Wes shouted to Eugene. "Have you found yours yet? And do you think it will run?"

"I've done worse to it," Eugene shouted. "But no I haven't found it."

"Well hurry up, we don't need anyone catching us!" Wes said impatiently.

"You are so full of wisdom, always!" Eugene shouted back. Before Wes could further berate Eugene, the tops of the impounded vehicles started glowing faintly. It was probably just a trick of the eyes. Except it didn't stop. The glow was now alternating blue and red. Yes, something was definitely illuminating everything blue and red. Wes's stomach sunk simultaneously with the *whirp* sound of a police siren turning on and quickly off. Wes ducked down as low as he could and ran to Eugene. The lights were getting brighter and the random *whirps* were getting louder.

"Fuck!" Wes shouted to Eugene just in case the latter wasn't already thinking that.

"I know!" Eugene said just as he spotted his beat up, smashed-in car in the very row they were hiding in. Without saying anything else, he pointed to it and they both took off running. They could clearly hear the sounds of the police car running. It was now parked and they heard the doors open. With no time to lose, they each opened a back door and climbed in.

"Get under the capes!" Wes said in a shout-whisper.

"Uh, if you're going to try to make out with me," Eugene started.

"We're gonna need more beer ha ha ha now shut the fuck up!"

Wes said with panic in his voice as he pushed Eugene under their costumes. From a nearby row, they heard footsteps. They didn't seem too close. But then the voice coming through the megaphone didn't sound very far.

"We know you two are hiding somewhere in this lot. We understand this is a very fun game." The words stabbed Wes's eardrums. Maybe not so much the words, but definitely the familiar voice.

"Holy shit, it's Evan Thomas!" Wes whispered to Eugene. "Does this town only have one goddamn police officer?!" The megaphoned voice continued.

"But now it's time for you two retards to go home. Okie-dokie?"

"Fuck, the prick knows it's us and called us retards!" Eugene exclaimed to Wes.

The footsteps were sounding closer. They were surely in the same row. Wes and Eugene huddled under the pile of capes and suit jackets. It was getting hot. Both men started to sweat. Where was all of the air? Were they suffocating? They heard another voice, this time not coming through a megaphone.

"Well, we've done all we can," Detective Wade Wadeler said to Officer Evan Thomas as he lit a cigarette.

"We sure did. It's in God's hands now," Evan said back. They were not good law enforcement officials.

"'Was it not my hand which made all these things?' Acts 7:50," Wade said. He was known to quote scripture. "The night is young, old friend. We now are out amidst the bats, junkies and prostitutes. And I have an idea involving all three."

Wade was not kidding. He was never kidding. Evan was about to agree when he noticed something down the aisle.

"Hey holdup. That's Eugene's fucked up car," he said to Wade as he noticed Eugene's fucked up car.

"Whose car?" Wade asked.

"Wes's little friend's. Remember? When I saw them today, they had just crashed this. And I want to know what was in the back. There was something weird about everything.

"But, Evan, don't you need a search warrant?" Wade asked. They both broke out into laughter. Okay, sometimes Wade was kidding. But not usually. They walked to the car where Wes and Eugene were buried in the back.

From inside Eugene's sweet ride, two grown men cowering under capes heard the voices, but not clearly. They did, however, clearly hear footsteps getting louder and louder.

"Dude, they know we're in here somehow," Wes whispered to Eugene.

"Maybe, but it's not like they're allowed to get in any impounded car they want. We have rights as citizens! They can't do whatever they--"

Eugene was interrupted by the sound of the driver's door opening. They heard someone get in. Even though all they could see was black, they laid wide-eyed and still. Neither of them dared to breathe. The passenger door opened and another person got in. Both doors shut.

"There's a lot of shit in this car," Evan said to Wade from behind the wheel. He was right. Aside from the pile of wonder in the back seat, the front was cluttered with Arby's wrappers, phone-charger cables, toothpicks, change and leaflets.

"There is a lot of shit in our collective consciousness," Wade said as he took a drag from his lit cigarette.

"Don't get all weird on me now, Wade," Evan replied. "I know cocaine makes you introspective. Hey, dare me to hot-wire this piece of shit?"

"Do you think it will even run?" Wade asked back skeptically.

"One way to see," Evan said as he ripped a bunch of cords out from under the dash.

Meanwhile, Eugene's sweaty face had become contorted as he felt a sneeze trying to build up inside him. To everyone's surprise, the car came to life.

"Perfect!" Wade exclaimed. "Now, we take this shitty car, find some hookers, get 'em to hook us, then bust 'em for hookin'!"

Evan and Wade high-fived each other, except the sound of their hands slapping together didn't make the familiar clap-sound they were used to. It sounded more like the sneeze of a human adult male hiding under a bunch of shit. They looked at each other. Wade caught a tiny glimpse of motion from the back seat. Evan nodded toward the pile and held a finger. Then two. Then three. Then in one fluid motion, Evan and Wade ripped off the layers of cloth revealing Wes and Eugene sweaty and red-faced curled up in the back seat.

"*What the fuck!*" Evan shouted. "*What!*" He said again. "*What the fuck are you guys doing in here?!*"

"We live here?" Eugene replied.

Everyone looked panicked except for Wade, who seemed surprised, but not fazed.

"Well boys, it looks like we've got quite a situation. I am inclined to believe you heard us talking to each other just now," Wade said calmly.

"We honestly didn't hear anything! We couldn't!" Wes said desperately.

"Especially about drugs and prostitutes!" Eugene added. Wes shot him a look that would frighten a grizzly bear, which as every good traveler knows, is the world's most powerful bear.

"Of course you didn't hear anything," Wade said as he slowly put his hand on his pistol. "You didn't hear anything because there was nothing to hear."

"Nothing to hear but hear itself," Wes heard himself say before he realized he was talking.

"Boy, I don' t know what in heaven's holy fuck that means, but I think you're on my team. Are you two on my team?" Wes and Eugene both nodded obediently.

"We are on you and your gun's team," Eugene told him steadily as he could speak.

"Well, that's good news, isn't it?" Wade said. "Unfortunately, my gun doesn't have a team. Now, Officer, how are we gonna do this?"

"Detective," Evan said to Wade, "they were obviously here trying to steal cars."

"And then what happened?" Wade asked his colleague.

"Well, from the evidence gathered, they saw us, panicked, and tried to attack us." Wes and Eugene shared a look. They didn't like what was going on.

"With what, Officer?" Wade asked.

"With this knife." Evan reached in his pocket and pulled out a small but effective pocket knife.

"Whoa, whoa, wait!" Wes's adrenaline was rising furiously. "We would never attack you!"

"Hmm, that's not what will be written in the paper tomorrow," Evan said. "Detective, what happens when two armed thieves attack officers of peace?"

"Well, it's likely that the officers of peace would have to defend themselves from the armed thugs," Wade said.

His gun was now out of its holster and in his hand which was steadily rising. The gun barrel stopped moving once it was pointing directly at Wes's face.

"Sirs, I'm going to have to ask you to exit the vehicle."

Wes put his hands over his head and did what he was told. There was no use arguing now. There was no use trying to reason. One can't reason with the unreasonable, with the corrupt.

"You too," Wade said, aiming his pistol at Eugene. Eugene grabbed a pair of the black leather gloves from his costume and put them on as he climbed out of the car.

"What the fuck are you doing?!" Evan shouted at Eugene.

"I'm..." he wasn't quite sure himself. "Thugs wear gloves, right? I'm providing evidence." It kind of made sense, at least to a coked-up crooked cop.

"Hey, good idea. Put all that shit on!" Wes looked confused and paused, giving Evan just enough time to shout *do it!* as he got his own gun out. Wes and Eugene each pulled on gloves, suit jackets, capes, and ski masks, though neither of them pulled the masks down over their faces.

"Now stand next to each other. Executions have order, gentlemen."

Wes and Eugene stood in front of the driver's side of the car. Evan and Wade stood in front of them about six feet away, each pointing a gun at a victim.

"Now, if you believe in a higher power, it might be a good time to get to know him or her a little better," Wade said as he vacantly looked into Eugene's surprised eyes. Surpreyes.

Wes was staring directly into the barrel of a gun. His eyes met Evan's, who was looking delighted.

"I will never have as much fun watching someone get shot as I'm about to have right now," Evan said in a low, intense voice.

His hands were surprisingly steady for someone high as fuck on cocaine. Wes didn't dare to move, though he wanted with everything he was to look at Eugene. He knew that there wasn't a chance he and Eugene could silently communicate an effective get-away plan through glances, but it might be nice for the last thing he would ever see in his miserable, wasted life would be someone he - for lack of a better word - cared about rather than someone who used to pee on his lunch.

And what a dreadful last thought for Wes to have before getting killed to death: Evan peeing on his things. But this was it. There was no time for him to think of anything more pleasant. Unless Eugene could think of a way to stall their impending doom. Now there was something pleasant: Wes considering Eugene being able to delay their deaths somehow. He obviously wouldn't be able to get them out of this bloody demise, but maybe him being an idiot could buy them another thirty seconds.

Wes's thought was broken by noise. It must have been a gun shot. This is it. Except, that was not what a gun sounded like. That was a voice. A human voice belonging to Eugene.

"Doesn't it make you sad that you'll never get to pick on Wes again, Evan?" Eugene spoke with confidence, to everyone's surprise. "Don't you have more of his things you want to pee on?"

Evan, who was directly in front of Wes, turned to look at Eugene.

"You know what, Detective?" Evan directed his comment toward Wade but didn't dare take his eyes off of Eugene. "I think I'll handle these two self-defense shots myself."

"By all means, Officer. It is your call." Wade lowered his weapon, though he didn't put it back in his holster. "If you think you can protect both of us from these two scumbags, then please save our lives."

"No, I'm serious. You pissed on his lunch at school. What better way to say 'fuck you forever' than to piss all over his stuff one last time before he meets his unfortunate demise?"

Wes's expression did not change. If this was Eugene's grand scheme to buy them another minute or so of life, he could do without it.

"I did have a lot of Coors before work tonight. Actually, I have been waiting to pee for like ten minutes," Evan said.

"Officer, when nature calls, you must answer," Wade encouraged.

Evan lowered his gun and began to unzip the fly of his uniform pants. Wes was in complete disbelief. He was too scared to be angry, until he managed to catch a glimpse of Eugene with the corner of his eye, who Wes could have sworn was smiling. Was this Eugene's last big joke? They're both about to get shot and Eugene's final hilarious gag was to get Wes urinated on once more? Eugene did have difficulty knowing when something is appropriate.

"Michael Westin, you truly are a piece of shit. And when I take a shit, I usually end up pissing on it as well."

Evan's voice was punctuated by the sound of a stream of liquid bapping against pavement. It seemed everyone was watching the stream as it inched toward Wes's shoes. Wes couldn't feel the stream hitting his black Converse sneakers at first, but being that they're cloth, his toes began to feel warm and wet as the yellow dick liquid - diquid - soaked into his feet and ran down the rubber soles.

Wes was truly about do die with pee-feet. What Wes didn't notice, and neither did Evan or Wade as they were both transfixed on the justice of the situation, was Eugene's hand slowly inching upwards. If he had wanted to, he could almost reach out and touch the pee stream from where he was standing. And he did want to. Not with his hand, but rather the small device his gloved-hand was touching.

Before anyone could notice what was happening, there was a loud *ZAP*, flash of blue light, and a scream from Evan as he went tumbling backward!

The device Eugene had been grasping was the taser he had left in his jacket pocket from this morning! Wes was starting to put two and two together and figuring out that Eugene, *brilliant* Eugene, had tased Evan's urine, sending the electric current through the pee-stream and up into Evan's penis! Wade was about to raise his pistol and fire, but before he could, Eugene triggered the electricity again and threw the peed-on taser in Wade's face, sending him screaming and hurtling backward as well!

"*Run!*" Eugene shouted to Wes, who immediately turned on his squishy shoes and bolted with Eugene leaving the two crooked cops writhing in electric pain on the ground.

Evan's penis was protruding out of the front of his pants, urine still trickling out and streaming down himself onto his crotch and legs. They ran out of the gate, which was still opened, passed the guard who was watching some other show on television having grown bored of watching the policemen, and down the road. After about five solid minutes of running, Eugene shouted to Wes, through his panted-breathing.

"Wes!"

"Yeah?" Wes panted back.

"Where are we running to?" Eugene asked.

"I don't know, Wes answered without stopping. "Our place isn't safe," he said. He was probably right but he wasn't sure exactly why.

"What about Bonnie's?" Eugene asked.

"I don't think so. I'm sure she's not too hard to track down. Those two probably remember us hanging out with her. Plus, do you really want to put her and Jeremy in danger?" Wes breathed deeply a few times and continued. "And I don't really want Bonnie finding out that we're the two idiots who beat up Jake Mortinburg this morning."

"We're fucked," Eugene correctly stated.

"We're fucked," Wes correctly agreed.

"We're fucked," they both said together and stopped.

They looked at each other and repeated it in unison again. *We're fucked.* They knew where they had to go, and it wasn't going to be fun.

Around a half hour later, the two men were standing on a porch looking straight up at a door. They looked at each other. Wes nodded toward the door, indicating that Eugene should knock. He shook his head. Wes's eyes grew wide and he gestured again. Again, Eugene shook his head. Wes knocked. The sound seemed to echo directly off of their bones. Eugene started trembling as they heard someone inside nearing the other side of the door.

Eugene took one step to start to run away, but Wes grabbed him by the arm and he stopped. The door slowly creaked open and there she stood. Her night-wear was worse than they had counted on. It was just so small! The folds of her body seemed to swallow any sort of strap that was keeping the ready-to-burst nighty in place. There was just so much... exposure.

Eugene gasped and shielded his eyes. She looked like a can of Pillsbury biscuits that burst open on its own, with dough escaping from inside the container from every place it could. A voice much deeper than it had any right to be spoke.

"Well." The sound made both grown men shudder. "This is a nice surprise. What brings you to my neck..." she paused for way too long, "of the woods?"

"Hi Joan." Wes said as evenly as he could. The two were looking at the porch. "We are in a bit of trouble. It's all a misunderstanding but we can't go to our apartments tonight." Joan bit her bottom lip, hoping that what she thought Wes was about to say is what he was about to say.

"Do you," Wes gulped, "have an extra couch or something we could crash on tonight?"

"An extra couch?" Joan repeated with a giggle. "No. I don't."

Eugene started to turn to leave again.

"But," she said lowering her voice even more, "there is always room at my inn."

"Oh mother-fuck! Are you kidding me?!" Eugene stopped pretending to be okay with any of this. "You don't have a couch?! Come *on*!"

"Don't be a dick to our gracious host, Gene!" Wes said. Joan beamed.

"But she's definitely going to rape us!"

"Joan, will you excuse us for a moment?" She nodded but made zero effort to give them any privacy.

They turned around in place and formed a two-man huddle. Wes spoke to Eugene in a hushed voice that was still completely audible to Joan.

"Look, this is a safe place for us to hide out tonight," Wes said.

"Safe? *Safe?!*" Eugene replied with no hush in his voice at all. "I really don't know what is worse at this point!"

"Well, what exactly is our alternative, Eugene?!"

"I don't know, whatever those two crooked cops will conjure up for us can't possibly be that bad. Death?" Eugene was starting to think not letting them get shot was a mistake.

"Do you know what I heard her tell Tom, the mail boy, once?"

"What?" Wes indulged.

"She told him, I swear to God, she said, 'You know the best way to avoid rape?'" Eugene waited for his friend to guess, which he did not.

"'Consent.'"

"Oh, wow. That is horrible on a lot of levels," Wes agreed, genuinely offended at this truly terrible statement.

"But we're here. Unless you have a better plan, we're going in."

Eugene was at a loss for words. Instead, he pleaded to Wes with his eyes. Wes turned around first to find that Joan had somehow managed to pull the top of her nighty down and the bottom up, revealing several more inches of pale, taut, pimply skin.

"Joan if it's okay, we'd like to stay here tonight with you," Wes said with a sigh.

She put a leg up and gestured for them to follow her. As she turned around, both Wes and Eugene were greeted with the sight of at least forty percent of her pajamas pulled into and up her butt crack. They followed inside and the door closed slowly behind them, creaking like an old, haunted house.

"Would you like a drink?" Joan asked once they were inside, not at all trying to hide the curious brown-yellow bottle of suspicious looking pills she was opening.

CHAPTER 6: Pickup Sticks

The sun was rising brightly in the sky. Birds chirped happy songs as they dug for breakfast. All over the city, people were drinking coffee, reading the newspaper, and getting ready for the day. But one house had a different story to tell. The front door opened and two men walked out wearing black dress pants, white short-sleeved dress shirts, neckties and black Converse shoes. They were pale and sweaty. Once the door was shut behind them, they looked at each other and then away.

"Let's agree now," Eugene said to Wes, "to never ever talk about what went on in there. No one knows. Ever."

Wes responded by leaning over the porch's handrail and vomiting into the grass below.

"Should we take this out on Jake Mortinburg?" Eugene asked his sick friend.

"Someone will pay." The men walked away from the house refusing to take another shameful glance at it. They turned to the right and walked, fearing they would never get far enough away.

In Detective Wade's office, Wade and Evan were not happy. They looked like absolute hell and had obviously been up all night.

"We need to figure out what to do to those pricks," Evan said to Wade in a cold growl.

"When I was four years old, my older brother had a roman candle," Wade answered. His eyes became vacant. "He also had a frog. I remember watching him take his frog and gently place it in the hollow part of a cinder block and light the roman candle. He threw the firework in the cinder block with the frog and held a piece of wood over the top, keeping the frog trapped inside."

He studied his fingers for a moment before continuing. Evan mimed shooting bullets at the wall.

"I can still see the colored light flickering out from the edges. The smell of sulfur. When the noise had finally subsided, he picked up the board and we looked inside." Wade looked back at Evan. "For an instant, the frog was perfectly preserved as a frog-shaped pile of ash. Then at once, the wind carried it away."

"I need your point, Wadeler." Evan was in no mood for this.

"When the electricity charged through my veins, I felt like that pathetic, helpless frog. I felt like I was not in control. I felt like a husk of a man. I want the two who caused those feelings dead. Dead like a crispy ash-frog." Wade had made his point.

"I know. Everything else gets ignored until we track them down," Evan said through gritted teeth.

"Have you looked up their addresses?"

"They're both dumbasses but I'm sure they know they wouldn't be safe at their homes." Evan was thinking harder than he ever had in his life. "And I'm sure they don't have any other friends around."

"They never did in school either," Wade pointed out. He then added as an afterthought "Except that blond girl with the tits." They both sat in silence before looking at each other.

"She was a loser, too. Do you think she ever moved out of town?" Evan's gears began to turn.

"Shit, do you remember her name?"

"Of course not," Wade answered. "But her name is definitely in our senior year-book. I'll look through until I find her. I'll absolutely recognize those jugs when I see them." Evan's face formed an evil smile.

"Then we have a lead."

*

Back at school, the protagonists were creeping behind a row of bushes that seemed to be perfect for hiding. The playground was completely still aside from a little bird hopping around at the bottom of the slide.

"Recess should start in just a couple minutes," Wes told Eugene.

"I know, I was here yesterday," Eugene replied. "I miss my taser."

"It was a noble sacrifice. I can't believe you totally tasered Evan Thomas in the dick!" Wes smiled proudly.

"I know and he was all 'Ahhh my dick' and whatever!"

Eugene laughed with Wes until they heard the bell ring a moment later. Children flooded out of the doors and into every corner of the playground. Eugene stood up. Wes grabbed his jacket and pulled him back to crouching.

"Give them a minute to justify what we're about to do," Wes whispered. Eugene nodded. "I don't even see Jake Mortinburg."

It was true, he was nowhere to be seen. Over by the swings, however, they saw their small friend Henry being held off of his feet by another boy.

"Move," Wes instructed. They crouch-ran toward the scene.

"I told you," the older boy shouted at Henry, "the swings are mine today! Stay off 'em!"

"They're everyone's! And you better put me down before those ghosts come back and get you!" Henry told him.

"They ain't ghosts! They're losers! And after the school hired those extra volunteers to guard the playground--"

"What volunteers?" Henry interrupted. "I don't see any out here!"

"They're inside getting instructions and stuff right now! Those two losers would have to be pretty dumb to come back today."

As the older kid spoke, a shadow formed on the ground in front of him and he heard a terrible impression of Christian Bale's Batman voice.

"Unlucky for you kid, I am pretty dumb." Wes pointed a finger heroically at Henry. "Put that younger kid down!"

Henry's face beamed with excitement until the older kid holding him by his collar threw him four feet into the grass as hard as he could.

"There, I put him down," the boy said in a mocking voice. What a shitty little asshole kid. Fuck this kid!

"Bad move." Wes picked the kid up by his shoulders and lifted him until their eyes met. "Where is Jake Mortinburg today?"

The kid answered by spitting in Wes's right eye. It dripped under his mask down his cheek. Wes's grip tightened as he thought about how to handle what he was feeling. He gently set the kid back down and repeated his question.

"He got expelled for our sweet YouTube video," the shitty kid announced. "He ain't even here today." Wes felt the spit glob reach his chin.

"So you and your trouser-snakes are going to play nice today?" Eugene asked.

"No, that means I'm the leader! The playground is *mine!*" said the Kid.

"You're sure?" Wes asked almost looking for an out. The little prick was not about to give him one.

"I'm gonna bite you!" the kid shouted unexpectedly.

"Not with a mouth full of spit," Wes said.

He slid his food behind the kid's legs sending the bastard to the ground, landing on his back. Eugene pried his stupid little bitchass mouth open and Wes hovered about a foot above him. After a second of moving something around in his face, Wes puckered his lips and a bubbly gob began to appear.

"That's not going to taste good," Eugene started to tell the kid.

"See, we were at this chick Joan's house last night and-"

He thought about what he was about to say and decided against it. This kid was only eleven years old, after all. He didn't need to be exposed to that filth.

The wad of saliva slowly descended downward until it was a hair's width from inside the struggling boy's mouth. There was a long, thin line of slimy liquid still connecting the gob to Wes's rank mouth. Then it dropped. Past the teeth and inner cheeks right onto the back of the kid's tongue. Eugene pushed his mouth shut forcing him to swallow. Assuming their work was done, they let the kid back on his feet. Before they could ask again if he was going to behave today, he was shouting.

"*Snakebite!*"

Kids started running toward the swings from everywhere. Some were members of the gang and others were kids hoping to see a repeat of the now legend that was yesterday. Wes and Eugene stood back-to-back and started beating every kid that got too close, which happened to only be Snake members. They were the ones who already had bruises.

Eugene back-hand-slapped a kid to the ground. One child charging at Wes was stopped with Wes's still urine-smelling shoe suddenly in his teeth. The kid started crying as he angrily picked up a rock and tried to smash it into Wes's mouth.

"Hey! You'll grow new ones! I won't, you dumb dick!" Wes shouted as he caught the kid's rock-hand and smashed it into said kids own belly.

"Fuck my cock!" Wes heard Eugene shout.

He turned to see his friend on the ground. Two kids had managed to knock him over and another was running at him.

Eugene grabbed a stick from the ground next to him and pointed it at the one quickly approaching him.

"Stupify!" he shouted.

The kid was not affected by the curse so instead Eugene jammed the stick into his opponent's side. This seemed to have pretty much the same affect, as the kid was now doubled over on the ground unable to move. Predictably, the carnage lasted only a couple of minutes before adults were on the scene. One by one, volunteer grown-ups hustled toward the swings. Wes was too caught up repeatedly slapping the kid that spit on him to notice until Eugene shouted.

"Wes! Adults!"

"*Oh shit!*"

*

Bonnie happened to be walking near her apartment door when she heard a knock. She had assumed Wes and Eugene would come by at some point today, but not this early in the morning. As she answered, her smile quickly vanished. Wes and Eugene didn't wear badges.

"Hello, ma'am." Evan's voice was not friendly, nor was it immediately familiar. But his face may have been. She squinted.

"Evan? Evan Thomas?" she said not hiding her surprise. "You're a cop now?"

"Yes ma'am," he replied.

"Makes perfect sense somehow. Can I help you two with something?" Bonnie was in no mood to pretend to be pleased to see them.

"Ma'am, we'd like to come in and ask you a few questions if you don't mind," Evan said in no mood to pretend to be pleased to see her.

"I guess."

She opened the door wide enough for them to walk past her and gestured to three chairs at a small table in the kitchen. Jeremy was in the living room watching television with toys in his hands. The only distinction to the kitchen being a separate room was the sudden lack of carpet. The three sat down at the table. Evan spoke first.

"Do you remember those two losers you used to be friends with in school?"

"I don't remember being friends with any losers," Bonnie started, "but my two best friends were Wesley and Eugene."

"Close enough. Ma'am, when was the last time you saw these two?" Evan asked.

"We got together yesterday," Bonnie answered honestly.

"Fucking knew it," Evan said to Wade. "Losers never branch out. Always stick with other losers."

"Evan, didn't you and Wade used to hang out in school?" Bonnie asked.

Neither of the men understood Bonnie's point and ignored the question. She went on anyway.

"Is something wrong with them? Are they in trouble?"

"I am the judge and jury of trouble," Wade finally said. "Evan is the bailiff." No one understood what that meant.

"So, yes? Do I need to bail them out of something or can I go back to my business?" Bonnie was losing patience.

"Is this your little man?" Evan nodded toward Jeremy, who was now standing on the couch.

"Yes. That is my son," Bonnie thought it was pretty obvious.

"And he's not in school today?" Wade asked.

"No, no he didn't feel well this morning." Bonnie swallowed. "I said he could stay home."

"Shame," Evan said, as the mood shifted. "What was wrong with the little guy?" Bonnie didn't like these questions, or their tone.

"Headache." She said, simply.

"Well that's too bad," Wade said trying his best to imitate human sympathy. "But I must say, the TV is up pretty loud for someone with a headache."

Bonnie looked at Jeremy who was now standing with his face half-an-inch from the screen.

"Jeremy sweety, turn down the TV," Bonnie said to Jeremy. He obeyed. Bonnie was smart enough to not trust Evan Thomas, and she didn't like where this seemed to be going.

"Ma'am," Wade said, "do you know that it's illegal to keep your child out of school for no reason?"

"There is a reason!" Bonnie snapped back. "His head hurt!"

"So you say," Wade said as he looked at Jeremy. "So you say."

"I would hate to have to investigate this," Evan said. "It's usually very stressful on the child. And on the parents. Speaking of which, I assume this boy's father, your husband, is at work?"

Bonnie wasn't wearing a ring and she knew a police officer and detective would notice that. Evan was a dick.

"No, he's at his house," Bonnie said with no apology.

"Divorced," Wade suggested.

"No, we were never married," Bonnie said.

"Adultery." Evan was stretching it. "I'm sure there's a story there. We can talk about it now if you'd like. We were planning to head over to where your pal Wes works, though. Except we don't know where that is. So I guess we'll stay."

Evan wasn't being subtle. Bonnie knew what he was getting at and instinctively knew she shouldn't send them anywhere near Wes. But on the other hand, she couldn't have them interfering with her and Jeremy's time together. Wes was clever and should have no problem handling himself. Bonnie's mind lingered on the phrase *handling himself* for a moment while she suppressed a grin as much as she could.

"He works in the office park on the corner of Marsh and Lund. Telescom."

"Then that's where we will be headed," Evan said as he stood up.

"I do hope your boy's head feels better," Wade said as he glanced toward Jeremy, who was smashing an action figure into his temple.

Evan and Wade stood up and walked out of the apartment with much purpose. Bonnie couldn't help feeling guilty, despite having decided that she didn't have much of a choice. That made her angry. Helpless. Fuck those two fucks.

She decided to call Wes and let him know that he should expect the unwanted visitors at work.

Wes and Eugene were about a mile away from the elementary school and at the moment appeared safe. They dodged and weaved through enough yards and alleys to lose the unexpected grown-up patrol that had chased them off of the playground. That didn't mean they should stop running.

"Who would have thought that a child's YouTube video would cause such a rise in playground security," Wes panted.

"Fucking Jake Mortinburg. The only thing I regret about today is not getting to kick his ass," Eugene said.

"I never expected to do so much running in my life!" Wes said as he grabbed his side.

"Shocker," Eugene unnecessarily stated.

Wes felt his phone vibrate in his pocket. He looked around and stopped running. They were in an empty service drive between a couple of buildings near the loading zone. When Eugene kept going, Wes shouted to stop because Bonnie was calling.

"We're talking calls during our getaway now?" Eugene asked sarcastically.

"Keep a lookout, dickhead." Wes said as he answered his phone.

"Hey Bonnie," he said still panting.

"Wes, oh my god, wait why do you sound so out of breath?" Bonnie said through the phone.

"I was just... working out," he lied.

"There's no way that's true, but moving on. Dude, Evan Thomas is a cop now and he was just at my apartment looking for you!" Bonnie told him frantically. Wes pretended to be surprised.

"Oh really? That's very weird!" Smooth.

"It *is* weird, Wes! He didn't say why he is looking for you." Wes was worried about her inevitable next question. "Do you know why he's looking for you? He had weird Wade with him too. He's a detective."

"Boy I sure couldn't tell you why Evan would be looking for me. Maybe because he is and always has been an irrational douche bag. And Wade? I thought that guy would be in prison by now. Or a priest. Both?"

"At any rate he knows where you work somehow and is headed there now," she guiltily told him. "I'd leave work if I were you. He can't be up to anything good."

"Oh shit! Yeah, we'll ditch work and avoid him. Thanks Bon," Wes said. Eugene's eyes widened as Wes hung up the phone and put it back in his pocket.

"What the fuck?" Eugene figured this question was broad enough to be answered with the information he desired.

"Evan and Wade went to Bonnie's apartment to find us and now they're going to Telescom!" Wes said in a panicked voice.

"What the fuck!" Eugene figured this statement was broad enough to convey the information he wished Wes to receive about how he was feeling. "So where should we lay low then? Do you think Arby's is open yet?"

"Did you hear what I just said? We have to get the fuck to the office!" Wes shouted as he started to head in that general direction.

"That is a worse plan than mine," Eugene concluded out loud. "If they catch us, they will kill us. Nobody likes getting tased in the dick. That's a scientific fact, Wes!" Wes stopped and turned around.

"Gene! Before we left work yesterday do you remember what we were doing on our computers?" Eugene realized he was busted.

"Look, I'm a lonely guy. I don't meet a lot of chicks and I guess you could call it a 'dry spell'..."

"No, I mean," Wes processed this information for a second. "Wait, at work dude? Come on. No, I mean our chat and that video of Jake Mortinburg. Do you know how easily a trained detective and police officer can see those things and trace us to beating up those kids?" Wes was frantic.

"You didn't leave it open on your computer yesterday, did you?" Eugene asked.

"No, but you know! Cops are like fucking wizards when it comes to looking through computers. Haven't you ever seen a TV show with a cop and a computer? And sometimes there's a guy whose job it is to just do that! A computer cop! We need to go back there and clear the history!" It was true.

"Huh." Eugene thought about this. "You are right. Well, I'll probably catch up with you later. Clearing a computer's internet history isn't a two-person job. And I totally have a coupon for a free Jamocha Shake with purchase of a regular roast-beef sandwich." Eugene pulled the coupon out of his pocket to make sure he still had it. As he re-read it to make sure it was still good, Wes snatched it out of Eugene's hand.

"If you ever want to see this coupon again, you'll come with me," Wes said over dramatically

"So you take hostages now, too? If you hurt one hair on that coupon I'll kill you."

"I was going to ask why it is covered in hair," Wes said suspiciously.

147

"I mean it's not like it's my hair," Eugene responded perhaps more suspiciously.

"Ew. Let's go."

Wes and Eugene started toward the main road.

"We don't have any chance of getting there first on foot. We're going to need a ride," Wes said as he held his hand up to hail a taxi. "What's even in a Jamocha Shake?" he asked after a minute of waiting.

"Well I've never made one of my own because Arby's seems to have it perfected," Eugene said. "But I assume you start with a jar of milk…"

"Wait." Wes couldn't let that go. "A jar of milk?"

"Well probably not the whole jar," Eugene said reasonably.

"No, I mean where on earth do you get your milk? Why does your milk come in a jar?"

"The fucking…" Eugene was looking for the word, "Milkman. The Milkman who brings my milk delivers it on my porch in a jar." Wes was rightfully skeptical.

"Nope," he said in a full show of skepticism. "That's not a thing."

"Moving on," Eugene said trying to finish his thought about how to make a delicious Jamocha Shake until Wes cut him off again.

"No moving on. You don't have a milkman. No one has a milkman because this isn't the 1950s. What does he look like?"

"You know I sleep in until eight minutes before work! I've never seen him before," Eugene said.

"And that haunting bit of information never raised any red flags? How much do you pay this guy?"

"I've never given him any money, that's ludicrous! How much do you pay the mail man for your mail?"

There were a lot of things about the world that Eugene didn't know. Wes was determined to get to the bottom of this but a taxi finally pulled up and stopped. They climbed in the back. The driver was a thin guy whose bald head seemed just a little too small for the rest of his body.

"Havin' a go, are ya then?" the driver said in a thick Manchester accent. Wes was thrown off for a second by the unexpected speech.

"Uh," Wes composed himself. "Corner of Marsh and Lund,"

"Eh?" the driver asked.

"Marsh and Lund!" Wes repeated. "And hurry!"

"All right, no need to nook your knickers," the driver said as he pulled back into traffic.

Wes and Eugene sat nervously and impatiently, because they were feeling nervous and impatient.

"This has been a weird couple of days, right?" Wes finally said to Eugene.

"Well not particularly, but--" the driver started to answer.

"I was actually talking to him," Wes interrupted as he nodded toward Eugene.

"Oh. Right. Fuck me, then. I'm just a driver, aren't I?" the cab driver said Britishly.

"No, that's not what I meant, it's just..." Wes was back peddling. "Why would I ask if you've had a weird couple of days? I've never met you before."

"That's right, no need to get to know somebody you've never met. You got too many friends as it is, right Mr. Popular?" the driver shot back.

"Yeah, why are you such a fuck-face to everybody, Wes?" Eugene asked. He then reached his hand into the front seat. "Hi, my name's Eugene. Nice to meet you." Eugene shook the driver's hand.

"Hello, then. Wasn't so hard, was it? Not bein' a wank. You could teach some things to your rude friend." Wes was in disbelief about all of this.

"I honestly didn't mean to offend you," he told the driver. "So did you have a weird couple of days?"

"Well, no, but you knew that already, didn't you? You're just havin' a bit of a chat for chat's sake. You don't really care. You never really did. That's the problem with this country, innit?" Wes rubbed his forehead with his hands. Everything that was happening seemed to be pleasing Eugene, who was immediately on the driver's side.

"Yeah! Wes is the problem with this country!" Eugene chimed in.

"But, it's not just him, it's the lot of you. Goin' around snubbing strangers, stealin' internet, beating up kids, and illegally downloading junk on the telly!"

"Tell me about it," Eugene agreed before trying out his own British accent. "It's all rubbish!"

He said sounding like a character from Mary Poppins. Wes's ears perked and reddened because he noticed the driver referenced the crime they'd been committing for the past two days.

"Wait, who is beating up kids?" Wes asked as though he'd never heard of such nonsense.

"You haven't heard? It came over my radio. The police are looking for a couple of blokes who went to this school this morning and gave some kids the old one-two, eh? Wasn't you blokes, was it?" the driver told them expositionally.

Wes and Eugene looked each other up and down. They were still in their costumes aside from having taken off their masks and sunglasses. How suspicious did they look? Did the driver know? He didn't because at this point he started laughing hard. Wes and Eugene both nervously joined in his laughter. The driver suddenly stopped laughing and the other two followed his lead. The car was slowing. No, it was stopping. Yes. It was now definitely stopped.

"Right. Out of me cab," the driver said.

"Wait, why? Because I wasn't polite to you? That's no reason to kick us out," Wes pleaded.

"Corner of Marsh and Lund. You were only two blocks away to start with. Out of me cab," he said. Wes opened his door.

"Oh, sorry. It's been a weird couple of days," Wes told him.

"Right, I don't need your whole fuckin' life story, Knobnose," the cab driver told him. "Fifteen quid."

He reached out of his window and Wes got out his wallet. He handed the driver a twenty-dollar bill and waited to

see if that was at all the right amount. The cab driver took it
and sped off.

"Did you hear that shit?" Wes said to Eugene frantically.

"Yeah, 'quid!' I don't know if you got a deal or ripped
off," Eugene said to Wes.

"Dude! If the driver heard about this shit, then the real
police are looking for us, too!" Wes shouted.

"Well, Evan is a real cop. Even if he is a dick," Eugene
replied.

"I know he's technically a real cop, but he certainly
doesn't go by the book."

"Neither did Shaft. And I'll be God-damned if I'm gonna
stand here and let you disrespect Shaft!" Eugene said.

Wes thought about arguing with Eugene or pointing out
that he had once again missed the point, but he was quickly
distracted by the sight of a police car speeding away from
behind their office building. His heart dropped into his
stomach. Literally. His four-chambered mammal heart
descended into his abdominal cavity and ripped through the
lining of his most important gastric organ and he died.

Figuratively. That didn't really happen but that's how he
felt inside. He figuratively felt as though that had literally
happened. Eugene, who hadn't noticed the police car, did notice

his friend suddenly falling over dead into a ball on the pavement. Figuratively. He noticed that Wes's face had suddenly gone pale.

"You look like your heart just sunk into your stomach," Eugene figuratively told Wes.

"I literally just saw what I assume to be Evan's police car driving away. Which means we're too late and they've already been here and found out everything," Wes said in defeat.

"Well, then there's nothing to do now except drink Jamocha Shakes."

"No. We have to go in. I want to know what they know," Wes said.

"Your logic," Eugene said, "is flawless."

Inside the office plaza, Lance was standing at Joan's desk trying desperately to ignore her gross cleavage. He looked angry enough already but when he saw Wes and Eugene approaching, he snapped in a furious rage of words.

"Wes! Why on earth were the cops just here looking for you?!" he spat.

"I don't know, Sir."

"You and Eugene are late *again!*"

"I know, Sir."

"Well? What do the two of you have to say for yourselves?!"

"We are sorry," Wes told him. Eugene nodded.

"Yes, we are sorry," Eugene piped in.

"Sorry? *Sorry?*" Lance's face was turning red. "I'll say you're sorry. In fact, you two are the sorriest losers I have ever had the displeasure of knowing! You are so fucking stupid all the time! I bet the reason you're late is because you forgot how to tie your shoes. Or, you saw a bird and tried to talk to it. I have never met two people who are of as little value as the two of you. No one on this earth cares about you! Not one person thinks you're worth any more than a big bowl of shit!"

As Lance continued to direct insults toward the two, Wes stopped hearing words. Instead, the sounds were turning into more of a hot buzz mixed with the faint whistling of a teapot in his head. The buzzing and whistling grew louder in Wes's ears. He didn't notice his hand was clenching. He didn't even notice his arm was raising. He was no longer aware of anyone else in the room other than Lance and himself. Lance. Wes had never really put together that something was wrong with Lance's face. His big, red, angry face was missing something. What was it? Oh, right. A fucking fist.

Pow!

Wes's punch to Lance's mouth sent him tumbling backward into the wall, where he slid down and fell to his butt.

Wes was immediately on top of him beating the ever loving piss out of his boss. Eugene and Joan watched motionless and expressionless as they watched kicks and punches pummel Lance for about a full minute-and-a-half.

When it was over, Wes stood up and calmly walked to his cubicle. Eugene and Joan looked at each other, and then watched Lance try to gather himself back to his feet. He shouted toward Wes, who was now out of the room.

"I'm pressing charges, Westin! I'll sue you for everything you've got! Joan? Joan, you are a witness!"

"A witness?" Joan asked.

"Yes, you saw the whole thing!" Lance shouted desperately.

"Saw what whole thing? I didn't see anything at all," Joan said as she dug her nail file out of her purse.

Eugene was stunned. He caught her eyes for a quick second and saw her give him a wink. Eugene was pleased and impressed. Lance stormed away to his office, trying to hide the fact that he was crying like a bitch. *Like a bitch!*

In Wes's cubicle, Wes was standing at his computer with his brow furrowed. Eugene walked in behind him. Wes addressed Eugene without taking his eyes off of his computer screen.

"I don't get it. There's no internet history. It's already been cleared..."

"So," Eugene said, "you just beat the shit out of our mean boss."

"But why on Earth would the police clear away evidence they need?" Wes asked out loud.

"You were all *'boom, pow'* and he was all *'Aahhhhhh'* and shit!" Eugene continued.

"It doesn't make any sense," Wes said as he walked out of his cubicle. Eugene followed, still speaking.

"I bet he wonders when you grew a pair." Wes led them back to Joan's desk. She was glad to see them back.

"Joan, did the police go into my workspace?" Wes asked.

"Yes, after they erotically asked me all about you and Eugene."

"What did you tell them?"

"I told them you two were naughty. They said they knew that. I asked them to tell me all about how they knew you were naughty." Joan unbuttoned a button from her ugly blouse. It was already pretty unbuttoned.

"Did they use my computer?" Wes back-peddled as he tried to make what he just said sound less suspicious. "I mean, it's not like I had anything incriminating on it or anything, but I wouldn't want them to think the gross things Gene looks at on my computer were from me."

"Hey!" Eugene exclaimed.

"Well, they wouldn't find anything in your internet history if they did look," Joan answered.

"What? Why? Does the company delete history automatically?" Wes asked, puzzled.

"No, I cleared it when I was done in there earlier," Joan said.

"Okay, good. Thanks," Wes said before he could comprehend what she was telling him. Then it started to set in his brain. "Wait. What were you doing in there?" Wes asked.

"A bit of this. And that," Joan said. She slowly lifter her fingers to her nose and gave them a gentile sniff. Wes and Eugene both shuddered.

"Ugh. Er, thanks. I guess," Wes said.

He walked away from the reception desk. Before Eugene could follow, Joan held her hand out to Eugene, inviting him to take a whiff.

"I'm going to walk away now, Joan. Because you are gross." As Eugene turned to leave, Joan shouted after him.

"You walk away now, but pretty soon you'll be dreaming of smelling my hand!"

Eugene caught up to Wes in the hallway, who was leaning on the wall with his face in his hands. This caught Eugene by surprise.

"You okay, Wes?" he asked.

"No," Wes said from behind his hands. "I'm about the most *not* okay I've ever been. I don't know what our next step is."

"Is it Arby's? Because my coupon..." Eugene was trying to break the tension and was mostly joking, but Wes dug the coupon out of his pocket and handed it to Eugene.

"Go to Arby's. Drink your Jamocha Shake. I think I have to skip town. Live life on the lam. Sleep in boxcars. Eat uncooked beans out of cans. Wear gloves with the fingertips cut off..." Eugene decided to slap Wes in the face.

"Wes! You're confusing being a fugitive with being a hobo!"

"Stop slapping me," Wes said.

"Stop being a bitch! Let's get out of here and figure shit out!"

"Where are we going to go? We can't move in with Joan."

"Well, what about Gary? We could hang out with him for a day," Eugene suggested.

"It's just starting to sink in how fucked we probably are," Wes stated. "I'm pretty sure we're going to end up jobless, in prison, and dead. Maybe not in that order."

"You're right, I will call Gary. Good idea, Eugene," Eugene said to himself as he got out his phone.

"Wait. Bonnie's Gary? Why?" Wes asked.

"Because he won't be suspicious. He is oblivious to everything that goes on around him and is just excited to have company. And plus, he's so nice."

"Sickeningly nice," Wes said. "But you're right. Have him take us somewhere. Anywhere away from here." Eugene dialed his phone and held it to his ear.

"Hi Gary, it's Eugene. Hey, could you do me a favor?"

Inside Gary's car, Gary was speaking a mile a minute. Figuratively. Wes was sitting in the passenger seat while Eugene sat in the back. As Gary spoke, the other two tried communicating with their eyes through the rearview mirror. They were not doing a good job. The words coming out of Gary's mouth were not making it into anyone's ears but his own for a solid four minutes. Wes gave up trying to silently talk to Eugene and rested his head against the window considering trying to find an answer to this question: *what the fuck?*

"So I guess that's how I ended up with this Toblerone," Wes finally heard Gary say. "Anyway, you never did answer my question." Wes snapped back to reality. Oh there goes gravity.

"What question, Gary?"

"Why are you two wearing capes?'

CHAPTER 7: Soapbox Derby

"We are auditioning to be in a play!" Eugene's cover story might have been genius. Wes and Eugene hadn't even noticed that they were still in their costumes. But they were. And they looked stupid.

"Oh of course! you're auditioning for Phantom of the Opera! I thought I saw masks," Gary said. Everyone was surprised except Gary. "I can take you there now! I was interested in checking out the audition anyway."

"Great, yes," Wes said. "Yeah our cars are out of commission and we needed a ride there."

"Where is the audition again, Gary?" Eugene asked, as unsuspiciously as he could.

"It's being put on in the auditorium at Jefferson High School this spring," Gary told them. Wes's brain clicked twice.

"Wait, Jefferson where we used to go?" he asked.

"You bet! Now if you want we can go straight there, or if you don't mind, we can pick up a couple of items that will put your mock costumes - mockstumes - over the top so the director knows you're serious!"

"Yeah, let's stop first. We can use the help." Wes was agreeing to buy time. Eugene leaned in and spoke softly to Wes.

"Does Gary think we're auditioning to be in a high school play?"

"He must," Wes said quietly back.

"Can grown-ups do that?" Eugene asked.

"They absolutely can't," Wes asserted.

"You know," Gary said without realizing he was interrupting, "I have the soundtrack right here." He picked up his phone from out of the very clean cup-holder. "What do you want to practice? What are you singing for your audition?"

"We, uh, haven't..." Wes started to say.

"Here's a good one," Gary said as he pressed a button. "Siri, play *All I Ask Of You* from The Phantom of the Opera."

The song started playing. This was the first person Wes and Eugene had ever seen use actually use the voice assistant on a smartphone. They felt conflicted about it. Gary began singing with Steve Barton as the character of Raoul, while telling the other two to join in when they were comfortable.

Gary then sang, in full volume, the entire first verse along with the recording by himself. He looked at them expectantly when it was nearly time for Christine's part. Wes started to clear his throat and prepare to try to fake sing along while simultaneously recognizing what a stupid position they were in. Just as he was about to sing along, he was surprised to hear singing from behind him.

"Say you'll love me every waking moment!..."

Eugene was unexpectedly belting out Christine's part in beautiful falsetto. Wes's eyes widened. An enormous grin spread across Gary's face.

"Turn my head with talk of summertime..."

As Eugene finished his verse, Gary joined back in with Raoul. Both expressed more passion than one would expect two grown men belting out Broadway hits to express as Gary wiped his left eye. Wes stared straight ahead out the windshield in disbelief.

"Love me, That's all I ask of yooouuuuu."

They ended their duet in perfect harmony. Wes slowly turned around and made eye contact with Eugene. Eugene gave him a look which seemed to say *Yeah? What of it?* and Wes gave him an approving nod. Eugene smiled.

"Gene," Gary said into the rear-view mirror, "I know it's unconventional for a man to play the part of Christine, but you'd have my vote if it were up to me. That was simply stunning. I can't believe I've never heard you sing before."

"I mostly just sing in cars," Eugene said back into the mirror.

Then at the same time, Gary and Eugene both saw something else in the rearview that made their full-hearts figuratively sink into the literal cavity under their ribs where the human heart beats. And that something was the flash of red and blue lights.

"Oh rats, the fuzz," Gary said.

Wes took one glance and then in one motion clambered into the back seat with Eugene, pulling their capes over both of them.

"You two also can't stand cops? I won't tell them you're back there," Gary said as he started to pull the car to the shoulder of the road.

Once he came to a stop, both the driver's side and passenger's side doors opened on the police car. Predictably, Evan Thomas and Wade Wadeler exited the authoritative vehicle and approached Gary's window.

"The boys in blue! Well, one anyway. What can I do for you two?" Gary was trying to sound friendly.

"*Boys?* The fuck you call us boys for, fancy pants?!" Evan shot back.

He meant what he'd said in a derogatory manner, but Gary's Dockers were pretty expensive.

"I just meant it as an expression. I know you are grown men," Gary said back, flatly.

"We are an expression of justice," Evan incorrectly stated. "Now I'm gonna need your license and registration."

Gary retrieved the requested documents from his wallet and glove box and handed them to Evan.

"I clocked you at 36 miles-per-hour. Do you know what the speed limit is on this street?"

"Oh, I thought it was 35. I apologize," Gary responded slightly confused.

"So what you're telling me," Evan said after taking a deep breath through his nose, "is that you knew full well the speed limit on this road is 35 and yet you were willingly driving upwards of 36?" Gary blinked.

"I guess, I--" Gary struggled to find words. "I was singing along to my favorite musical and I guess I didn't notice my speed."

"Musical? Like what, a opera?"

Evan's failure to use *an* before a word starting with a vowel made everyone confused and sad. It sounded like it took more effort to say but he wasn't doing it on purpose. Eugene, listening from under the capes in the back seat decided then and there that every time he could remember, he would stop using the word *an* where applicable to bring tension and uneasiness to conversations.

"Well, it's a musical about an opera," Gary told him.

Evan stared at Gary for about a full minute while he tried to sort out the information he had just been given and what to do about it. The fact that he was wearing sunglasses and stood perfectly motionless added to the air of discomfort. Frankly, Gary still wasn't over the whole grammar situation.

"Sir, I'm gonna need you to exit the vehicle," Evan finally said.

Gary opened his door, unbuckled his seat belt and stood facing Evan and Wade. Evan then hit Gary with a club. Gary shouted.

"Shut the fuck up. Now I don't know where you get off zipping along singing with a musical about a opera or whateverthefuck out in Madison, Wisconsin, but in my city, ain't nobody got time for that kind of faggotry."

Everyone except Wade winced at his unexpected use of such a discriminating word.

"This here is God's country. You know what the Bible says about faggots?" Gary was aware of most religions' views toward homosexuality but stood motionless. "Tell 'im what you told me, Wade."

Wade slowly took a cigarette out of his pocket and put it between his lips. He lit it and took a long drag. He then cleared his throat. Wade was known to quote scripture.

"Genesis: chapter 19," he proclaimed in an impressive manner. "Lot prepared a feast for them, complete with fresh bread made without yeast, and they ate. But before they retired for the night, all the men of Sodom, young and old, came from all over the city and surrounded the house. They shouted to Lot, 'Where are the men who came to spend the night with you? Bring them out to us so we can have sex with them!'"

It was at this point that Evan spit on the ground in disgust. Wade continued.

"So Lot stepped outside to talk to them, shutting the door behind him. 'Please, my brothers,' he begged, 'don't do

168

such a wicked thing. Look, I have two virgin daughters. Let me bring them out to you, and you can do with them as you wish."

It was at this point that Evan and Wade high-fived.

"But please, leave these men alone, for they are my guests and are under my protection.' 'Stand back!' they shouted. 'This fellow came to town as an outsider, and now he's acting like our judge! We'll treat you far worse than those other men!' And they lunged toward Lot to break down the door. But the two angels reached out, pulled Lot into the house, and bolted the door. Then they blinded all the men, young and old, who were at the door of the house, so they gave up trying to get inside"

While Wade was giving his scripture lesson, Eugene couldn't take any more of what he was hearing without whispering-shouting about it to Wes.

"*I fucking told you*! Do you hear him keep saying the 'f-a-g' word? That guy is a gaycist!"

"Yeah I, wait, what did you call him?" Wes whispered back.

"A *gaycist*! You know, like racist but for gays," Eugene explained.

"Yeah I get it, but we already have a word for that. It's called 'homophobe'."

"Bullshit! 'Homophobe' implies being afraid of homosexuals. He's not afraid, he's a idiot!"

Wes thought he just heard Eugene forget to use *an* in front of *idiot* but assumed it was because they were whispering. Either way, it made him even more uncomfortable somehow.

"That's an excellent point and I am adding your word to my lexicon," Wes said back.

Outside the car, Wade continued his speech.

"Leviticus 18:22: Do not practice homosexuality, having sex with another man as with a woman. It is a detestable sin. Leviticus 20:13: If a man practices homosexuality, having sex with another man as with a woman, both men have committed a detestable act. They must both be put to death, for they are guilty of a capital offense." Wes was enraged.

"You hear that shit? He's quoting Leviticus now! That's like the worst one!"

"Leviticus was a dick, everyone knows that!" Eugene acknowledged.

Their whispers were suddenly interrupted by more shouts and screams. Wes and Eugene knew what was going on and didn't want to peek through their cover. They could hear the sounds of a club beating against a human body, the screams from the victim and the war-like grunts of the attackers. They knew Gary was getting the Christ beaten into him.

"We have to do something!" Wes told Eugene.

"I know! But you know they'll kill us this time!" Eugene correctly stated.

"If only we had disguises," Wes said sarcastically as he slipped on his mask. Eugene followed suit.

"Okay. If we can throw our capes over Wade and Evan, maybe the surprise of sudden blindness will be enough of a distraction to pull Gary in the car and speed the fuck out of here."

"Your plan is to throw a sheet over them?" Eugene asked.

"Look, it's that or do nothing while Gary gets beaten! I'm going to slowly count to three. By two, let's have them in our vision. On three, we shove the door open and move. Got it? Here we go: one."

Wes and Eugene started to very subtly lift their heads.

"Two."

They pulled away the cape that was obstructing their view of the beat down. But before Wes could say *three*, it was apparent they had incorrectly deduced the ruckus outside. The information that their eyes gathered and sent to their brains that had trouble accurately interpreting as reality was suddenly apparent: Wes and Eugene weren't hearing Evan and Wade beating up Gary.

Gary had grabbed the club and was absolutely losing his shit on the two gaycists! Wade was on the ground in a fetal position while Evan was trying to stand back up onto his feet, only to have his own club repeatedly strike his temple. Gary whipped the club into Wade's ribs and proceeded to continue to rain hurt on Evan with his fists. Evan eventually gave up, not able to yield any defense and fell on his side next to Wade. Gary gave one final and forceful kick to Evan's stomach before straightening his cardigan.

"You know what?" Gary asked the two bloodied-masses on the ground. "I'm not gay. I'm bisexual. For 35 years I've struggled with that and have never fully admitted it to anyone or myself. So thank you for helping me through this struggle."

Wes and Eugene stared silently, continuing to barely peek through the back-seat window under their black capes. Gary started to get back in the driver's seat of his car, but stopped and turned back toward the two men on the ground.

"Also, all that stuff you took the time to memorize? It's irrelevant. All made up. Somebody made all that shit up a long time ago. I'm half gay and full atheist. So I guess that makes me a gaythiest. You guys just got your balls bloodied by a gaytheist."

The club in Gary's hand fell carelessly to the ground. Eugene couldn't take it and had to whisper-shout.

"Holy fucking shit, that is the most badass thing I have ever seen!"

"I know and then he throws a *portmanteau* in there?! Gary fucking rules, dude!" Wes whispered back to Eugene. They giggled to each other until they heard the car door shut. The tires screeched and they were zooming away.

The two in the back sat up and removed their cover and masks. Wes didn't know what to say. This is usually where Eugene would say something stupid to break the silence, but he was being annoyingly quiet as well. After a moment, Gary switched on *Music of the Night* and sang beautifully along as though he hadn't just beat the living fuck out of two particularly awful human beings.

"This one's my favorite of the male songs," Eugene said to Gary from the backseat.

"Oh it's so good!" Gary said. The two sang along until the song was over.

"Gaytheist." Eugene stated. Gary grinned. Wes also grinned.

"Gary," Wes said, "We're really sorry."

"For what?" Gary asked.

"A lot," Eugene said.

"Those cops..."

"I know," Gary interrupted. "I'm probably going to go to jail. But you know what? If that's what it takes to defend yourself from the ignorant hate-spewing rants of vile people, then it was worth it. I don't expect you two to cover for me."

"No, that's not it at all!" Wes said. "Those two cops are looking for us because we overheard them talking about getting hookers or something. They are what we call 'crooked cops' and they are assholes. They probably targeted you looking for information about us. If they did any investigating at all, they can easily link you to Bonnie, who they linked to Eugene and me."

"And we definitely will cover for you," Eugene added. "I'll lie under oath. What the fuck even is a oath?"

"Interesting. Then just now in a way I was protecting my son?" Gary asked.

"Absolutely," Wes said.

"How much time do you think we have before they get on their feet and hunt us down?" Gary wondered out loud."

"I dunno, maybe an hour?" Wes speculated.

"Perfect," Gary answered. "That still gives us plenty of time to hit up the thrift store and tweak your costumes before getting you two to the auditions."

Wes had all but forgotten about Eugene's clever lie of auditioning for a play. He momentarily considered telling Gary the truth about everything before realizing that Gary might interpret their heroism as putting Jeremy in unnecessary danger. Wes kept his secret to himself with no intentions of getting Gary's thunder brought down on him. Wes looked at Eugene, who he could tell was going through the same motions in his head. Eugene opened his mouth, but upon seeing Wes shake his head, he closed it without letting any words out.

Gary pulled his car into a spot in front of the local thrift store and got out. Wes and Eugene followed suit and the three men entered the shop. The slut working behind the counter offered an insincere greeting to the men without taking her eyes off of her phone. It occurred to Wes that he had no idea what they were looking for.

"I have no idea what we're looking for," Eugene said, immediately after Wes had formulated that exact thought.

"I literally was just thinking that!" Wes figuratively said.

"I think what would really set you two apart would be canes. We should find canes. And maybe broader hats." Gary took off down one aisle and wes followed.

175

Eugene approached the easy girl who worked there. She spoke to him without looking up.

"So you guys are probably going to prison, huh?" she said with as much emotion in her voice as a Dalek's. Eugene, who would not have understood that analogy, tried not to sound surprised by her question.

"I dunno, whatever," he replied coolly. "What?"

"I assume you are the two fucks all over the news for sneaking onto a playground and kicking the shit out of kids. Unless it was another pair of dudes who came in here a couple days ago looking for disguises to rough up some children. I believe what you said was you were going to 'bring them as close to death as possible.'"

"Oh right," Eugene said. "Yeah that's us. Should I flee?"

"No I'm not going to call the cops. But frankly, I'm surprised you're not in jail yet. Didn't you do it like twice or something?"

"The police force in this town hasn't impressed me," Eugene said. The corners of the slutty girl's mouth turned upward slightly.

"In fact, they're probably on their way for us right now. My new hero over there just beat the shit out of a cop and a detective for being gaycists. And the other night I tasered the same cop in the dick."

"That's pretty cool I guess," she said.

She hadn't realized that Eugene saying those outlawy things had made her legs spread apart. But she did notice that it was making her super wet. Like *super* wet.

"Yeah. I gotta go. We're getting canes to look more like the Phantom of the Opera."

"So are you auditioning for that today?" the girl asked.

"Nah, just pretending to want to audition," Eugene said as he walked back over to Wes and Gary.

The girl started fantasizing about making out with the Phantom's fucked-up face. She seriously had some issues.

"So it shouldn't take all night if you want to hang out later," Eugene said pretending he had some confidence, which he did not.

"I have another job after this one," she said out loud. But in her mind she added *blow, hand and rim.*

"Double-dipping, huh?"

One might think that she might have found and enjoyed the sexual innuendo in that expression, but she didn't. She thought it was lame and it dried her right back up.

"After that the only thing open is Arby's," she said.

"Shitballs, we're totally going there later! I've got this coupon—"

"We found canes," Wes said, inadvertently interrupting Eugene.

He held two canes up for Eugene to see. As Eugene walked away from the counter toward Wes, he started talking.

"That girl who works here knows everything," Eugene said to Wes.

Wes dropped both canes.

"No, she's cool though. She said she wasn't going to call the cops or anything."

"When you say 'everything,'" Wes started to say.

"Yeah, no, everything. And I just told her about Gary's deal. So yeah, no, she knows everything."

Eugene hadn't meant to say *yeah, no* at all, let alone twice. He considered making that his new thing, but he was still sorting out this whole *a/an* deal.

"Cool. Well, that sucks. We should probably go then." Wes started to move for the door.

"We should probably get to the auditions anyway," said Gary, who was half-listening. "I'll get the canes, you guys can wait in the car if you want."

178

Eugene followed Wes to the exit. Just as they were almost out the door, Eugene shouted back at the girl.

"Thanks, Daria!" and immediately turned to see if Wes thought that was funny. He didn't.

"Dude she totally looks like Daria. You know, from Daria!"

"I know she does, Gene," Wes said through tight lips. "But it's not as funny making fun of her now that she knows all this incriminating shit about us."

As he said this, they both turned and looked back through the window at her, who flipped them off.

"Yeah, no, we definitely need her on our side." Eugene said.

They got in the car and instinctively pulled their capes over their heads and bodies.

*

In the interior of an unmoving police car, two very bruised and very angry officers of peace sat silent. Wade sat with his head against the passengers seat head rest with his eyes shut, hands in lap. Evan's bloody hand was covering his eyes.

The police radio randomly sounded commands, requests and static. The noise was actively ignored.

"Officer Thompson and Detective Wadeler, please report your status to--"

The sound stopped abruptly as Evan calmly reached and turned off the radio. They sat in silence at the side of the road for another full minute before Evan finally spoke.

"Detective, I can't remember another time I've been this angry. Somebody is going to go down in the crossfire. And it ain't gonna be us."

"Don't say 'ain't', Officer. It makes you sound like a cunt," Wade calmly replied. "And the trick to curbing your anger is to focus the entire spectrum of your negative emotions on one target. In this case two. Eugene and Wes are not going to make it out of this alive. That's a cold, hard fact. That alone is all of the reassurance I need to remain on point. When I'm looking at two blue faces, eyes cold and vacant, it will all have been worth it. Frankly Sir, I am a fan of the hunt. Not just the kill."

"I am a fan of the kill and then celebrating with more kills. And blow. And hookers. And killing them." He absently started stroking his pistol.

"First thing's first. Wes and Eugene definitely have to die first. After that, then probably the faggot. Then, that bitch and her son. I don't know how they're involved with this bullshit

180

but I know they are. I'll probably off her son first in front of her eyes."

The tone in Evan's voice was a lot less hyper than it had been.

"Obviously, you shoot her little bastard in front of her, make her watch the life leave his tiny body, point out that it's because of Wes and Eugene, let her sob for a few minutes and then shoot her too?" Wade asked.

"That sounds about perfect."

The two men didn't smile, but something about them seemed happier, or at least more content with their situation. Evan turned the police radio back on, started the engine, flipped on the lights and siren and sped off into town.

CHAPTER 8: Revelations

"This place sure brings back some memories," Eugene said to Wes.

"Yep. All of them terrible," Wes replied.

They were standing on the sidewalk in front of the elementary entrance to Jefferson Public School. Gary had dropped them off for their "auditions" later that afternoon. The auditions were to take place at 3:30. Gary had suggested taking them there two hours early so they could run lines and be comfortable. It made perfect sense.

"Remember when you used to get beat up here like every day?" Eugene asked.

"Yep."

"Sometimes twice?"

"Yep."

"Sometimes by girls?"

"Yep."

"It's too bad we don't know who the current bullies are here at this school," Eugene said.

"What do you mean?" Wes asked.

"Well you know. If we knew who the bullies were at this school..." Eugene trailed off looking for the right words. "I mean, we are in our costumes. Afternoon recess used to be at 1:45. Do you think this school would change that shit?"

"Oh I get it," Wes said. "You're thinking about branching out. Like we should take our special brand of community service to other schools."

"I was mostly kidding, Wes. You beat up Jake Mortinburg and his goons because they were ruing the life of you best friend's kid. I mean, we don't really have anything personal against the fifth-grade shit-head assholes at this school."

"Personal?" Wes asked hotly. "I have something personal against *all* bullies! Plus, I don't give a fuck! Do you give a fuck Eugene?! When did you start just giving fucks?!"

"No, I don't give a fuck," Eugene replied.

"That's right! We don't give a fuck!" Wes retorted. "And we've got some time to kill. Let's go to the playground."

The two started to pull their masks down as they headed around the back of the school.

Finding themselves once again unsuccessfully trying to conceal themselves behind playground bushes, Wes and Eugene waited for the recess bell to ring.

"It should just be a minute," Eugene said out-loud.

"Some shitty little piss is about to have his life changed," Wes said back unexpectedly.

"Jesus, you're sure wound up today. I guess I'm not surprised. We have had quite a time. Hey, are you ever going to address what happened in the office?" Eugene asked.

"Gross Joan was covering her own tracks. My computer was clean. Well, figuratively clean anyway."

"Yeah, no, I meant that thing you did to Lance's face. Broke it. What about that?"

"He had it coming," Wes said.

"You're right, but he's had it coming for years. To date, that was the only time you've ever legitimately stood up for yourself. Well," Eugene paused, "to someone over the age of ten." Wes had no response. "Do you think you can summon that hidden rage again and apply it to the likes of Evan Thomas?"

"'The likes of?' What are we in the '40s?"

"I don't know why I fucking talk to you," Eugene said.

His next thought was interrupted by the sound of the bell ringing and a swarm of little kids raging onto the playground. Almost immediately, Wes spotted a child of about nine-years-old holding what appeared to be a first or second-grader up by the collar.

"Right," Wes said as they crouch-ran to the scene. Wes addressed the child in his low, grunty timbre.

"What the fuck are you doing to that little kid, Little Kid?!" The child was visibly shocked by Wes's use of cussing.

"You better put him down, you cunt-sucking twat!" Wes shot Eugene a disgusted look over that.

"Dude, don't say the 'C' word to a kid." Eugene was glad he did it, approval or not. The slightly older kid was confused, but channeled his confusion into confidence. He shouted back at the two.

"I want his lunch box!" he belted as he let go of the smaller kid only to then punch him in the stomach.

This triggered an incredibly vivid flashback in Wes's mind's eye. Wes saw through his eyes a quarter-century ago being surrounded by mean kids and felt his California Raisins lunch box being ripped from his grip. He felt tiny and angry. He shook it off and rejoined the present, being big and angry.

The smaller child, now doubled-over on the ground, was lifted to his feet by Wes. He ran away as soon as his feet hit the dirt again. Wes then picked up the other boy and held him directly up to his face. Nose to nose, Wes spoke to the child.

"When I was a kid, pieces of shit like you picked on wimpy kids like me all the time. I always dreamed of beating the life right out of them, but I was too small. Just like that first-grader you were just fucking with."

The boy spit a huge gob at Wes. It hit his nose and slowly dripped down. Once reaching the tip, it stretched and started to fall to the ground much slower than gravity usually works, maintaining a connecting line of saliva and mucus to Wes's nose. It finally snapped, and joined the rest of the spit on the ground, leaving Wes's nose gleaming with unwelcomed moisture.

"Dude," was all Wes could say through his pure rage. His grip on the little prick tightened.

"You probably shouldn't have done that," Eugene said.

"Now you are going to feel what it's like to be beat up by someone bigger. I'd say it's for your own good, but as it turns out, it's just as much for my good."

The feeling he felt in his office earlier was coming back. His fist was clenching and his arm was raising back. Here it comes. This kid is done.

"Put that child down!"

The old, raspy voice sent a chill straight into the bowels of both men.

"Who are you, and what on earth are you doing on my playground?!"

"Holy living Christ," Eugene breathed.

Wes turned around dramatically. What he saw were two glowing-red eyes peering through the tiny slits of the scaly, reptilian skin covering the face of a straight-up demon. Figuratively. But age was not on the side of Ms. Caldwell, the very same recess lady who worked there when Wes was in school.

Wes, losing interest in the child he was still clutching, threw him to the ground. The kid scampered off. Wes approached the old woman, staring in disbelief.

"Who the hell are you?" she said to them.

"We've met before," Wes answered

"God damn, you were like a hundred years old when we went to this school twenty years ago!" Eugene exclaimed.

"Listen here, Recess Lady. I've been recently justifying getting vicarious revenge on people who have wronged me in the past. And one time you made me eat a sandwich that was dropped on the ground."

Even through her cloudy, expressionless eyes, Wes could see that the figurative wheels in her brain were literally turning.

"But it hadn't just been dropped on the ground, had it Michael Westin?" Eugene gasped at her saying his full name. "It was covered in another boy's piss, wasn't it?"

"You made me eat it on purpose! It wasn't about wasting food! It was just to be a bitch!" Wes shouted in her face.

"Piss was too good for you, boy! I'd have made you eat a shit sandwich if I could have," she replied in a frail, mean voice.

"Ha. Shit sandwich," Eugene repeated.

Wes swung his arm back fully intending to punch the false teeth right down her stupid throat. He swung. But before his fist could connect, he felt something deflecting it. Ms. Caldwell had blocked his punch! On top of that, Wes suddenly felt the stinging blow of a karate chop in between his shoulder and his neck! He fell to his knees in disbelief.

"You think I could deal with shitty little kids all day for seventy-two years without being able to fight, bitch?" She said towering over Wes.

"I guess today *isn't* the day to stand up to people older than ten," Eugene pointed out. Wes got up and took another swing, but it was again stopped, this time by Eugene's hand.

"Dude. Little kids are one thing. They heal like Wolverine and we're teaching them lessons about respect. But an old fucking lady? Let this one go. She sucks." Eugene was starting to make sense.

"That's right, Wes. Listen to your friend. He knows when to run away like a pussy. He always has."

"You old cunt! I will kill you and murder your family if time hasn't done that already!" Eugene charged at the old cunt but Wes blocked him and held him back.

"No, Gene. This isn't your fight."

Wes threw a connecting punch into the recess lady's stomach. He was surprised how deep his fist sunk into her baggy old skin. She spat and fell backwards while managing to kick her foot into Wes's jaw sending him tumbling backwards. They both landed on their backs looking up at Eugene.

"That was amazing!" he said to both of them.

Wes scrambled to get up. He was able to charge Ms. Caldwell and knock her back down before she was back up on her feet. He pinned her down and slapped her repeatedly in the face. She managed to grab his hand and bite it as hard as she could. Wes screamed.

"*Fuck*! What are those fake teeth made of?!"

He tried to rip his hand back, but the teeth clenched harder. When he finally pulled his hand hard enough to escape, her dentures came out as well, flying several feet away from them. The recess lady took Wes's surprise as an opportunity to knock him back down and jump on top of him. She held his face in place and shouted at him.

"Look at me! Look what you did!"

The words came out through her loose-flapping gummy mouth, with plenty of blood and saliva. And a significant amount of foodstuff that had squished itself between her gums and dentures. She bent down as far as she could and shouted.

"*Look in my mouth!*"

She opened wide. She pulled Wes's mask up from covering his face. Wes couldn't help but look. It was bad. She got right in Wes's face with her mouth open until she was touching him with it. He felt her soft, moist and yet prickly mouth against his cheek. A steady stream of drool was pooling between her gums and lips, and it was all carelessly leaking onto

Wes. She rubbed her flappy open mouth along his face. It was as if she was gently massaging her gums against him.

Wes was weirded the fuck out.

"Wes! Is..." Eugene couldn't believe what he was seeing. "Is she *eating* you?!"

"Ugh, no!" Wes shouted, along with other groans and grunts. "I don't know what the fuck is happening! But it feels like someone put a baby octopus on my face!"

"I've never seen anyone do this before, Wes!"

Eugene was no help. Then with little warning, Wes vomited. Since he was on his back, most of it stayed relatively close to in his mouth, but some shot into Ms. Caldwell's mouth. It didn't seem to faze her as she slurped up the sick like a rubber vacuum cleaner eating a plate of ambrosia.

"I threw up and she ate it!" Wes shouted to a thoroughly weirded out Eugene.

"That was throw up?!" The recess lady shouted back. Her drooly, pukey mouth flapping loosely as she spoke. "That's disgusting!"

"What did you think it was?!" Wes frantically shouted back.

"What is this lady?!" Eugene screamed.

Apparently, ingesting someone else's bile didn't agree with the recess lady and she rolled off Wes. She then immediately started throwing up. Wes wiped himself on his sleeve and quickly pulled his mask back down, concealing his face once again. He stood up next to Eugene. Once Ms. Caldwell's body was finished rejecting everything she'd put in it, she laid still on the ground. Eugene cautiously approached her. After visually scanning her up and down, he kicked her in the ribs.

"Just to be a bitch," he said. Wes fist-bumped him.

"What kind..." It was hard for her to get words out, "of people beat up an old woman?" She finally asked. She was out of breath and nutrients.

"You're no woman," Eugene said. "You're a evil demon monster who somehow escaped the red dick of Satan himself to reign terror over the likes of innocent children."

"'The likes of?' Again?" Wes said.

"You know why everyone was mean to you guys?" the recess lady asked. She had curled up on the ground in front of them, still coughing and spitting.

"Because they were dicks," Wes answered.

"No." The sound she then made was similar to a human laugh, but not quite. "It's because you never did anything of value. You two. Are worthless. Always have been. All you and

192

your little friends did at school was stand around and make cynical comments about everyone and everything. You thought you were the most clever and funny people on earth, but really it was just annoying." She coughed again.

"Yeah?" Eugene replied. "Well, you're a bitch."

"Huuuuge bitch." Wes added.

"See? You're still doing it. Everyone hates you. It's a good thing you have each other because no one else in the world will ever put up with you."

Eugene took this opportunity to kick her again. This time instead of a thuddy-crunch, it made a pop. Then a scream came out of her mouth.

"MY HIP!" she shouted.

Wes and Eugene looked at each other. Had they gone too far? Probably.

"Hey Ms. Caldwell," Eugene said.

"What?" she croaked.

"Back in school, all the kids knew about your hysterectomy. And they judged you for it."

"You fucking slut. I hope you live another hundred years with no womb," Wes piped in.

Now they had definitely gone too far.

"You boys know you're going to jail for this, right?" she asked them. Without a beat, Eugene replied.

"You know you're probably going to die within an hour-or-so, right?"

"Probably," she said. "So let me die in peace."

"Not quite," Wes said as he unzipped his pants.

Eugene knew what was coming. A dick. That's what was coming. But not like a dick cumming, not like that. Like, a dick was to come as in arrive next sequentially in the order of events presently unfolding.

"As much fun as it was to break your old-as-fuck body, we are not even. You made me eat urine."

And there it was: a dick had come. But a dick had not cum, not like that. It was exactly as Eugene had suspected this whole time. Wes aimed his own floppy dick at the broken old-ass bitch on the ground and unloaded his entire bladder onto her wrinkled, dirty face.

"This got gross," Eugene told him.

It wasn't until Wes was done urinating on the old woman that they all noticed that they had been completely surrounded by the schoolchildren, who seemed shocked.

"See what happens when you pick on people?" Wes shouted, before grabbing Eugene and running the fuck away.

CHAPTER 9: You Think She's Pissed?

Bonnie was trying to read a book. She knew how to read just fine, but it had been a weird couple of days. Jeremy was playing with his action figures next to her on the couch. Well, he wasn't so much playing with them as he was making them violently abuse each other and breaking them. It seemed like smashing them together wasn't quite enough. They were out to destroy one another, and Jeremy was the omniscient being observing the carnage. Bonnie had tried to ignore it for some time, but it was getting pretty out of hand.

"You've been awfully rough with your toys lately. Remember when you made them figure skate?" She asked the way a mom who just doesn't get it would.

"No! They don't skate anymore! Now they're all super heroes, like those brave men from my school who came to save us," Jeremy told her gleefully.

"Those men were not heroes, Boy." Bonnie replied with figurative ice in her veins.

"Yes they were," Jeremy pleaded. "Jake Mortinburg got his ass handed to him just like this!" Jeremy pretended that one of the toys was biting the other toy in the face. The sound he made while reenacting the grizzly scene was unpleasant at best.

"It's still never okay to hit someone. You understand that, don't you?"

"But they didn't just hit them, Mom. They had super powers. Lasers came out of their fingers just like that guy in Star Wars!"

"His name is Emperor Palpatine," Bonnie told her son like a smug asshole, "and no they didn't. That kind of thing isn't real. Don't mythologize them to me, Buster."

"They *did*! I saw it! They were all '*ZZZZAP POW*' and-" Jeremy continued to list several onamonapias while throwing all his shit around like a little prick.

196

"And then the skinny one was all 'Ahh fuck my cock' and Jake was all 'You lanky garbage-'"

Bonnie interrupted her son in that moment. Something was triggered inside her brain. She felt like she needed a safe space. If this was a movie, it this would be the turning point where she started to figure everything out. There would probably be one of those rad shots where the person gets closer in the frame but the background gets farther away. What even is that, anyway? It probably has something to do with the camera moving forward on a track while zooming out with the lens, or vise versa. One can't always decode Hollywood magic. But this wasn't a movie. Although it would make a very, very good movie. *Box Office Hit*, they'd say.

"Jeremy, what did you just say?"

"Uhh," Jeremy was stalling because this question seemed like a trap. "Oh, whoops. Sorry, Mom, I cussed again."

"That doesn't matter. Tell me what you just said when those two toys were fighting." This still felt like a trap to Jeremy, but he complied.

"The skinny one said 'Fuck my cock', Mom."

"So he's the skinny one. What's the other one like?"

"He was sort of fatter and taller. Just a bigger man, really. He couldn't run very fast. He seemed clumsy. Actually, they both seemed sort of clumsy for super heroes."

"That's because they're *not super heroes*! I already told you that!" Bonnie screamed.

Her hair was suddenly askew like when someone in a movie shouts something at another character and they're disheveled out of nowhere. But this wasn't a movie. She had mentally put all of the pieces together, rejected the outcome, tore the pieces back apart, tried to put them back together in *any* other order, realized she was forcing it, tore those pieces apart, and put them back together in the inevitable way she didn't want to believe, all in the matter of four and a half seconds.

Jeremy stopped everything he was doing. He didn't know why he was getting yelled at but it made him feel sad and confused.

"I'm sorry sweetie. I don't mean to keep spazzing out on you," she said to her poor little bastard son. "I have to make a phone call."

*

Wes and Eugene were standing out front of the school that they were just behind. It seems like they would have run farther away from the horrific scene they caused out back than merely escaping to the other side of the building, but there it is. No one was around front because the commotion was all in the back. So logically it checks out.

"I feel like maybe I overreacted when I peed on her face," Wes factually stated.

"This has been fun, Wes, but I think I'm done with this game. I think we got all of the star coins."

Eugene of course was referencing the wonderful world of Super Mario, wherein once one successfully saves the princess, one can still go through and play the levels again finding new hidden treasures. One of the last things to accomplish is finding all of the hidden star coins. Once completed, the game is truly over. If this was a movie there would probably be a quick shot of a "Game Over" screen, depending on what type of movie it turned out to be and who was directing.

"Yeah," Wes replied. Because what else does one say in this situation?

Without hesitation, the pair of them removed their costumes. They were left standing in white v-neck undershirts, wrinkled suit pants, and shoes. As they held their ex-identities in their arms, it was unclear what the next step would be. Wes gestured toward the bushes with his head.

"Hide this shit in the bushes? That's so cliché." Eugene said.

"You're cliché." A fine comeback if there ever was one.

They pushed their disguises into the decorative shrubbery of the garden right in front of the school. Eugene then heard his stomach growl.

"Fuck's sake, is it just me or is it hungry out? I think the only thing left on the plate for today is a roast beef sandwich on mine. On my plate." Eugene was right.

Before Wes could find some reason to yet again break Eugene's heart over a fucking Arby's sandwich, his phone rang. He held up a finger to signal to Eugene that his phone was ringing and he was intending to answer the call. But Eugene had a pair of working ears and was able to deduce the pending events as soon as he heard the ringtone, like every other goddamn human being in the country. Wes's phone told him he was getting a call from Bonnie. He answered.

"Hey, what's up, yo?"

He hadn't even gotten out the *yo* before the sound began pouring directly into his brain. It was Bonnie, for sure. Specifically, it was Bonnie screaming and screaming and screaming at Wes. If this was a movie, it would probably be a scene where the sound from the phone was like a sped-up chipmunk voice for comedic effect, depending on the tone of the movie and the director. But this wasn't a movie, and Bonnie's screaming fit was so loud that Wes yanked the phone from his ear. Eugene could clearly hear that she was angry.

"Do you think she knows?" he cautiously asked Wes like a stupid idiot. Wes gave Eugene a look which was meant to imply that he thought Eugene was being a stupid idiot.

"*Wes, I cannot believe you two!*" were some of the first discernable words ripping through the tiny phone speaker.

"What were you thinking?!" were some others. "You clearly *weren't* thinking! Beating up *children*?! Little kids?? You're both beyond fucked up! You *must* know that! I *cannot* believe I wasted my life being friends with you two! Had I known this is who you'd become… I may have expected this from Gene, but Wes? *You*?! You're better than that! I expected more out of you and I don't think it's unreasonable to think your best friend won't be a *child-abusing psychopath!* I don't want to talk to *either* of-"

Wes's finger absentmindedly fell onto the bright red *end call* button on his phone. The screaming stopped. The silence started. Silence was good. There hadn't been nearly enough of that lately. After nearly a whole minute of stillness and silence, Eugene broke it.

"You think she's pissed?"

Wes gave Eugene the same look from before, which was meant to imply that he thinks Eugene is a stupid idiot.

"Yeah. Sounded pissed," Eugene correctly surmised. The figurative wheels in Wes's literal brain started metaphorically turning.

"I don't know how in the holy fuck she found out. Do you think anyone else knows?"

"No," Eugene confidently replied, "but that's based entirely on arrogance."

"Don't you get it?" Wes rhetorically asked. "If Bonnie knows, then that means people other than the two of us know. And if other people than the two of us know, we have to get the fuck out of here."

Wes's phone started ringing again, still in his hand from a moment ago. He looked at the screen and saw that it was Bonnie again.

"Dude, she's going to be mad at me forever about this one."

"Bitches be spendin'." Eugene of course was right. Bitches do be spendin'.

"There's only one logical thing we can do now that we've done all this illogical bullshit."

"*Finally!* This is going to be the best roast beef sandwich ever eaten by anyone."

"Fine, Eugene. Go to Arby's. I'm going to the police station to confess everything."

Wes's words landed in dumbfounded ears, along with the continual ringing of his phone. Eugene looked at his friend like he was a stupid idiot. He then slapped Wes in the face. Wes in that moment had had enough of that, announced that he'd had enough of that and slapped Eugene several times back with both hands.

"*Stop. Slapping. Me. All. The. Time!*"

"Fuck, dude, okay!" Eugene got these words out and Wes stopped hitting his friend. "You have honestly and truly lost your fucking mind. And as much as I usually love watching someone descend into the depths of space madness, you have to come to your senses and get your shit together."

"Me?!" Wes declared. "I *have* come to my senses! And do you know what? I'm tired of being everyone's punching bag. I'm tired of pussing out. And I'm tired of beating up kids."

This statement shocked both of them.

"And I'm in love with Bonnie! There. I said it. I'm going to nut the fuck up and get to the police station and take responsibility for the horrible shit I've done lately. Then maybe, just maybe, hopefully, she'll talk to me again someday."

Wes's phone continued to ring again in his hand.

"Fucker, you can talk to her right now if you hit 'answer'," Eugene said.

Wes remembered that he was holding an annoying ringing phone. He then manned up and answered. Without a second of hesitation, he held the phone up to his face and began to grovel.

"Bonnie, look. Yes it was me who beat up Jake Mortinburg. I couldn't stand the idea of Jeremy going through life *at all* how I went through mine. Was it a bad idea? Probably."

He could hear Bonnie trying to get a word in, but he didn't want her to start chewing him out again before getting his point across so he continued with no room for interruption.

"But I'd do it again a hundred times! You don't need to yell at me anymore because I'm going to the police station right now to confess everything. I'll take my punishment and-"

Bonnie was impatient and started shouting over Wes's awesome speech.

"*Shut the fuck up* and listen! *Do not* go to the police! They are corrupt!"

This was not news to Wes or Eugene, who was impolitely eavesdropping. Bonnie continued more calm than she'd been after a deep breath.

"Listen. At first I was going to call you to bitch you out for the most stupid thing I've ever fucking heard of in my life. And I still don't exactly know how to handle this situation. But then I got a call from Gary."

"Gary?" Wes asked. "We just saw him. What did he say?"

"He's…" Bonnie's voice quivered. "He's lying in a ditch next to his car!" She broke into hysterics. "Wes, two cops followed him, pulled him back over, dragged him out of his car and shot his kneecap out!"

She got the sentence out just before the uncontrollable sobbing.

"Are you fucking kidding?" Wes replied. "Do you know where his is?"

Bonnie was able to stop crying for a few seconds to get some desperate words out.

"He's not far from our old school. I don't know what he was doing over on that side of town! I am scared to leave my apartment!"

"Well, it's a good thing you called a super hero. Click."

It wasn't a good time to do the *click* bit again. In fact, it further worried Bonnie and she started sobbing all over again. So Wes actually hung up the phone.

"Dude," he directed at Eugene, "we gotta go. Those gaycist cops just hate-crimed Gary."

*

Behind a dusty old billboard on a dusty old dirt road on the edge of a dusty old town, there was a dusty old car. In that dusty old car sat two dusty old law-enforcers. Except they weren't dusty. They were bloody. Because earlier they had gotten the living daylights beaten out of them. But they felt better now. But not physically. Physically, they were in a lot of pain. They felt better now because they made someone else feel worse than how they currently felt. Spoiler alert: it was Evan and Wade who were in the dusty old car behind the dusty old billboard on that dusty old road, and they shot Gary in the dusty old kneecap and left him in a dusty old ditch. And they felt smug as shit about it.

"That fancy boy will think twice before being so fancy next time," Evan stated.

"When I was nine, I saw my first pair of pumps. I'm sure I'd seen them before in my life, but it wasn't until I was nine that I really noticed them. The elegance."

Wade paused and adjusted his nose. Partially because it was misaligned due to his previously mentioned savage beating, but also because of the amount of cocaine he'd just put into it. Even adjusted his nose for those two same reasons and also one additional reason. The additional reason had to do with the phenomena that occurs when one person makes a gesture and another person subconsciously mimics the gesture without realizing it. No one knows what this is called.

In that moment, it occurred to Evan that he has loved every story Wade has ever told him; that he hangs on every word as he waits for the exciting conclusion. But not this time. He watched Wade's bloodied, man-mouth making the words come out of it that are always so interesting. But not this time. Something was telling him to stop Wade's mouth. With his own mouth. Without over-thinking it, he leaned in and pressed his lips onto Wade's. Their lips embraced into a cocktail of blood, saliva and sweat. Evan could taste Wade's memory. And cigar smoke. They tenderly went at it for a baker's dozen of seconds before the radio on the police dashboard had the nerve to interrupt their passion.

"Attention all units!" the voice on the radio predictably announced. Evan and Wade jumped back with a start. "We have a-" the voice paused for a second or two. "Actually, no code number could fully sum up what has happened. Two grown men in ski-masks were just seen beating up an old woman on the playground of Jefferson High School. These two are most likely the same-"

Click. No one said *click*, but the action of Wade turning off the police radio made an audible click.

"Jefferson High School," Evan said to Wade. "Isn't that just down this dusty old road from here?"

"It's just down from my butt," Wade surprisingly replied.

"I love your mouth on mine. You know what else we might love?" Wade stopped listening, but Evan didn't know that and continued his thought. "It might be fun to go fuck up these two guys. They've been causing quite a ruckus in this dusty old town and we'd be heroes if we brought them in."

"I want to find, murder and cremate those two swines who tasered us."

Even assumed Wade was associating Wes and Eugene with the playground bandits but he wasn't. He just hadn't been listening.

"That's a great idea," Evan said. Then he realized something and became excited. "Hey, I just realized something!" he said excitedly. "I still have that taser! Let's get warmed up by tasering those two idiots at Jefferson and then tonight we'll celebrate our hero status by murdering our old school nemesis."

Wade liked the sounds of this and wondered if what he wasn't listening to a moment ago was this good, but didn't care enough to ask about it. He just gave Evan his answer:

"It's on."

CHAPTER 10: Shit Got Real

Gary was in rough shape. Wes and Eugene ran to the best of their abilities. It was literally as fast as they could. What they saw in front of them on the ground was Gary holding his bloody knee, keeping pressure on the wound. His car was half in the ditch in front of him. He had apparently ripped the sleeve off of his button-down shirt and had it tied tightly above the wound. His cardigan was next to him. Wes and Eugene both independently noticed the bulging bicep of Gary's now exposed left arm. His face was dirty and wet from tears, but furrowed in an angry-looking way that was foreign to his face.

"Why did you tear your sleeve off?" was the first thing Eugene said.

"What?!" Gary said breathlessly

"He asked why you tore your sleeve off," Wes told him in a helpful manner.

"I…" Gary struggled for words. "I needed to cut off the circulation to my leg so I didn't bleed to death!" he screamed.

"Right, I get that," Eugene continued, "but you took off your cardigan to rip off your shirt-sleeve. Why didn't you tie off your leg with your cardigan?" Gary looked surprised.

"Because, it's my favorite cardigan and I didn't want to get blood on it!" It was a very nice cardigan. It had some argyle in there.

"Forget the cardigan, we have to get you to the hospital!" Wes said.

"You're right! Gary's white as a jar of milk!" Eugene said.

As much as he wanted to, Wes determined it was not the time to ask a few more of the hundreds of questions he had about this milk situation. Eugene bent down and grabbed Gary from under the shoulders. Wes, in an effort to not touch Gary's legs, awkwardly bent over him and grabbed Gary's hips. They lifted Gary off the ground. The sounds Gary was making were not what one would describe as pleasant. It made Eugene feel weird. They shimmied Gary into the back seat of his car. No one was comfortable about any of this. Then Eugene had a notion.

"Wait, shouldn't we call a ambulance?"

Wes thought about this. It seemed like they should have called an ambulance. He also didn't know why Eugene saying that made him feel so gross.

"Well," Wes said, "I mean he's already in the car."

"Right, but shouldn't he be on a stretcher?"

"Hmm. Gary, would you rather be on a stretcher?"

Gary looked at them as though he was trying to communicate an answer without using any words. This sort of non-wordal cue was lost on Eugene.

"Wes, I think we need a ambulance." Wes involuntarily shuddered at that sentence. Before he could agree, the two of them noticed the sound of a loud siren in the distance. It was getting louder. In a few seconds, an ambulance pulled up next to the scene with its lights flashing. A Paramedic hopped out of the vehicle.

"Where the victim?" she said to them. "I was told there was an injured man in this dusty old ditch."

"Do… you guys take calls from the future?!" It was the only way Eugene could make sense of what was happening.

"That seems like a very efficient system!" Wes said.

"Is the woman here who called 911?"

Wes and Eugene put it together in that moment that Bonnie had of course called 911.

"You're a fucking idiot," Eugene told Wes.

"*Sirs!*" she shouted at them. "Is there an injured man here?"

"We…" Eugene didn't want to admit to her that they'd put him in the car without thinking. "We put him in the car without thinking," he said.

"It's been a weird couple of days," Wes added.

The paramedic opened the door to Gary's car. He smiled and limply waved to her, because he is very polite. She opened the back door of the ambulance and pulled out a stretcher and rolled it over to the car and gestured for Wes and Eugene to help. The three of them awkwardly hoisted Gary out of the car and onto the stretcher. Then they lifted the stretcher into the ambulance.

"Thanks," the paramedic told them. "I don't think I could have done that without help."

"Speaking of that," said Wes, "Isn't there usually a team of you to do shit like this?"

"Usually yes, but it's been a weird couple of days. The normal driver is pouting because his catfish-"

"Jesus Christ, how long is this story?!" Eugene impatiently interrupted.

"Right, I should get him to the hospital anyway," she sheepishly said as she dug her heel into the dirt.

No one ever thinks she's interesting. Maybe someday she'll find Mr. Right.

"Do you two want to accompany him to the hospital?"

"Nah," Wes said.

"Fair enough."

The paramedic hopped back into the ambulance and sped away, lights and sirens a-blarin'. That's an expression. Once the vehicle was out of sight, and it was just the two of them standing by that old, dusty road, Wes spoke.

"This is pretty bad."

"Shit got real," Eugene said.

"What did I say to you about using that phrase?" Wes asked.

"Not to be so real?" Eugene said and then laughed.

"What's our next step?" Wes asked.

"I dunno. Arby's and a movie?" Eugene asked. Wes thought for a moment.

"Is anything good out?"

"I dunno," Eugene said.

While they were pondering 42, they heard other sirens in the distance. It was a police car. They non-wordly agreed to stand and watch this police car go by before making any decisions. The car was going too fast for them to see, but if they had seen into it, what they would have seen was Evan's head attached to the body controlling the car. They would not have seen Wade's head, however, because it was buried in Evan's lap. Because Even had his penis out and Wade was fellating it, thus obscuring his head from view. After a minute or so, Wade popped up his head.

"Jefferson School is just up here," he said.

"How did you know that?" the coked-out Evan asked.

"I always know. *Always.*"

Wade cryptically replied as he put his head back down into Evan's lap. The beat up police car pulled up in front of the school and came to an abrupt stop. The two terrible human beings inside of it got out. They looked around suspiciously for clues. That's just what people need sometimes. Clues.

"These perps are obviously some kind of psychopaths," Evan said.

"The brain is a fascinating machine to say the least," Wade thought out loud. "What's in that bush?"

What was in the bush in front of the school was none other than some clues! Just what they needed. They managed to pull out a pair of hats, ski masks, capes, sun glasses, and gloves.

"Well well well," Wade predictably and satisfactorily said. "Looks like we found some disguises."

"Where did they come from?" Evan asked.

"From where did they come," Wade corrected as he licked the hats. "They're fresh. What do you think about doing some undercover work?"

"What do you mean 'they're fresh?'"

"Taste this."

Wade held the hat to Evan's face and Evan's tongue peeked out of his mouth like a nervous turtle's head. Wade rubbed one of the hats against the tongue.

"I don't know what I'm supposed to be tasting," Evan finally admitted.

"I say we put these on. My theory is that they belong to the suspects," Wade stated. "Oh these guys are good."

"Why would we wear their disguises?" Evan asked.

"Do you know how a sociopath's brain works?" Wade answered a question with a question, which is rude. "They ditched their costumes in such an obvious place because they want to get caught. If they see us wearing their disguises, they'll get angry because they'll think we are out to poach the fame and glory for their crimes."

"I like these hats," Evan said.

Wade was wrong, of course. They ditched their costumes in the bushes in front of where the crime took place because they're stupid. Wade and Evan sorted the pile of clothes and donned the outfits.

Gary's car was zooming down the road. But Gary wasn't in his car. By now he was at the hospital. His car was being driven by none other than Wes, with Eugene by his side in the passenger seat.

"I don't want to use the word 'lucky' in this situation, but I'm glad Gary left the keys in his ignition," Wes said aloud.

"It's lucky we were there to keep his car from being stolen," Eugene said. "He owes us! Plus, now we have a getaway car."

"It's not a getaway car, Gene."

"What are we using it for?" Eugene asked.

Wes didn't answer because he doesn't care for rhetorical questions. The car pulled into the apartment complex where Bonnie lived. Wes wasn't convinced that it was a good idea to go there right now, but they really didn't have a choice. Eugene had brought up Arby's again several times on the drive. Wes knew deep down that a Jamocha Shake sounded very very good, but here they were.

They went up the stairs to her apartment. She is balled up on the couch. Her mom and dad went down to Charlotte. They're not home to find us out. The last three sentences are from a song, not a book. They knocked on Bonnie's door and then used the key Wes had to let themselves in. An alarmed Bonnie jumped up from the floor where she and Jeremy were playing and walked up to Wes as he spoke.

"Bonnie, we got Gary on course to the hospital. He's probably healing already. He should be fine, but then that's an assumption based on—"

His sentence ended with a very painful slap in the face, compliments of Bonnie. He didn't entirely process what happened before she started screaming at him.

"You son of a bitch!" she shouted, not caring that she just swore in front of her son. "I *can not* believe you two! Get out of my apartment. Now." She was serious.

"Bonnie I was just trying to give Jeremy a better childhood!" Wes pleaded.

"Get out," she reiterated.

"Look I know we made a mess but-"

"*Get out!*" Bonnie pushed Wes toward the door. "I can't talk to you right now!"

"Am I allowed to stay or is this a both-of-us-have-to-go kind of thing?" Eugene awkwardly asked.

"Get out!" Bonnie said as she pushed Wes up to the door.

"I'll probably go too then," Eugene said. "I have a milkshake to drink so…"

Bonnie pushed Wes through her open door and into the hallway. She proceeded to slam the door as hard as she could in his face. The door barely caught the tip of his nose. Eugene, who was still in the apartment, calmly walked up to the door, turned the knob and pulled it open, walked through to stand next to Wes and slowly closed the door behind him.

"Girls are weird," is what Eugene thought an appropriate thing to say would be. Wes agreed, but ignored the statement.

"Bonnie please," he said to the door, "Let me back in."

"Go away, Wesley."

That's what her voice from behind the door said. Words were forming inside Wes's brain. They arranged themselves a covert mission to bypass his filter and come straight out of his mouth.

"But I love you."

Wes was just as surprised to hear that as both Bonnie and Eugene were. They stood there in that moment for an eternity. Figuratively. But literally for 28 seconds. 29 seconds later, Bonnie replied.

"What?"

This was an opportunity to edit/undo what had just happened. Bonnie was giving him a chance to take it back. But in that moment, Wes used something he wasn't used to using: his balls. A pair figuratively grew in the literal scrotum hanging under his wiener. It was a feeling he'd felt once earlier that day and he went for it.

"I said I love you."

He asserted with the confidence of regular-sized balls. Bonnie said nothing for another 28 seconds. An observer would have noticed the time and wondered if she was waiting exactly that long on purpose by timing it with a stop-watch. Or more than likely, a stop-watch app on a smartphone.

"Why didn't you tell me that ten years ago?" Bonnie asked exactly 29 seconds later.

"Because up until today I was a bitch," Wes told her.

"He's right," Eugene added, "he was a bitch. But dude, Bonnie! You should have seen him earlier at work! Our stupid boss was all 'uhh duhh I'm a dickhole' and Wes was all *'bam, pow, kretsch'* and that jerk was all 'ahh waahhh I suck' and-"

Wes motioned for Eugene to stop saying words.

"Bonnie, I never had any nerve to do anything in my life. Not stick up for myself, take any risks, go for any dreams. Besides, why would a beautiful woman like you ever want a schmuck like me?"

"You are a schmuck," Eugene added.

"I was just lucky enough you talked to me, let alone be my friend. Why would I want to risk ruining that with romance?" Wes knew he'd just asked a rhetorical question, but all bets were off at this point.

"You know," Bonnie said 16 seconds later, clearly not timing herself with a stop-watch or stop-watch app on a smartphone, "I always thought of you like a brother." Wes winced at the sharp words.

"But a brother I would have sex with."

Wes and Eugene looked at each other in confused disgust.

"That's not something I expected to hear," Wes said.

"Brothers... with benefits?" Eugene asked.

"That came out wrong," Bonnie said as she searched for what possible words could fix what she just said.

"Bonnie, do you want to have sex with your brother?" Eugene asked.

"No, I want to have sex with Wes!" she finally blurted out.

Wes's face figuratively lit up. He literally smiled a large, excited smile.

"Then you should let him back in," Eugene said.

"I didn't mean right now," she said as she opened the door.

The men want back through the door and Wes went right into Bonnie's arms. He then grabbed her face and pulled it to his and passionately kissed her like he'd never kissed a woman before. Which, maybe he hadn't. Eugene wondered if the recess lady gumming her sloppy mouth over his face counted as kissing, which it didn't.

"That is not how you kiss a brother," Eugene told them.

Jeremy had enough of grown-up time and went to play on the iPad in his room. Everyone forever ignored that Bonnie mentioned having sex with her brother in front of her son. She pulled away from the kiss.

"Shut up, Eugene. I'm still very very pissed off at both of you. Did you put together yet that you're almost certainly going to get caught and go to prison?"

"No, yeah," Eugene said.

"So that's why the cops were here looking for you then?"

"Yeah," he repeated.

"No," Wes said. "That's not why they were looking for us. We were trying to get one of our cars out of the impound lot and we heard them talking about breaking cop rules with drugs and prostitutes. That's why they are after us. Nobody knows that it was us behind the vigilante thing."

"Nobody figured you guys out?" Bonnie asked suspiciously.

"Nope, not one person," Eugene started to say as his mind wandered toward the slut who just sold them canes and Wes's face getting thrown up on again.

"Two people. At least. The girl at the thrift shop who looks like emo Tina Fey and the recess lady at Jefferson."

"Wait. Jefferson? Our old school?" Bonnie asked as she figured out their tangled web of terrible was larger than she thought.

"Yeah she definitely knows," Eugene said.

"We should maybe go back there and make sure she doesn't talk," Wes said. He wasn't sure if even he knew what he meant.

"Wrong. We should move to Mexico and fiesta!" Eugene suggested.

"Bonnie, we are terrible at being vigilantes. Ideas?" Wes asked.

"I don't know if going to where everyone will be looking for you two suspicious men is a good idea."

"You're right," Wes told her, "but sometimes we need to take risks! I can fix this. I just need to talk to Ms. Caldwell."

"The new Wes isn't really about making good choices," Eugene told them.

"Eugene, it is stupid, dangerous, and irresponsible for you two to go back there!" Bonnie said.

"Hey Bonnie?" Eugene said.

"What?"

"I don't give a fuck!" Eugene told her.

"We don't give a *fuck!*" Wes repeated.

The two men high-fived. Wes grabbed Bonnie and pulled her toward him giving her another great kiss on the mouth. Then, they turned and ran out the door like two men with a plan, which they didn't have.

"Wait!" Bonnie shouted. They didn't.

"I love you too, Michael," she said out loud, but they were too far away to hear.

Chapter 11: A Bunch of Bees

Outside Jefferson School, two men stood wearing black suit jackets, hats, ski-masks, and sunglasses. They were dressed an awful lot like maybe how playground vigilantes might dress, except their pants were blue. The kind of blue you might find on a police uniform. It was a suspicious sight, to say the least.

"You know I never listen to our police radio, right?" That was not the voice of Wes or Eugene, but that of Evan.

"You're a busy man," Wade's voice replied from behind the other ski-mask.

"Did the chief say something about sending other officers here?" Evan's voice asked.

"You know for a fact that I *hate* being confused with a stenographer. *I hate it!*" Wade's voice replied loudly.

"You are so full of life!" Evan's voice exclaimed.

"Now, if I know anything about being a psychopath, it's that they are definitely still somewhere nearby monitoring the grounds. They'll see us in their costumes and confess because they want the credit for their actions." Wade's voice made a lot of sense.

"And once they do that, we'll arrest them, read them their Miranda Rights and let our legal system decide their fate." Evan's voice was quiet after that for around four seconds before both voices started laughing at the thought.

"You know Evan," Wade's voice started to say, "I really thought we wouldn't have any more bodies to burn this month. Other than prostitutes, of course."

"It's been a good month, buddy!" Evan had a different definition of the word *good* than a lot of people.

"Now, if I remember right, and if not much has changed in twenty years, there is a perfect hiding spot for us near the sand box. It's behind the school on the playground."

Even was so out of his mind, that he didn't realize explaining that a sand box was part of the playground was redundant. Wade gave him a nod and the costumed men took off for behind the school just as a car pulled up in front of the building. Two other men got out of that car. They were not wearing awesome costumes, just white v-neck t-shirts and suit pants.

"So after beating up and pissing on the recess lady, you're just going to casually ask her to cover for you if the police start asking around?" Eugene asked like an asshole.

"This may come as a surprise, but I haven't really thought this through," Wes said back. "I was thinking about maybe telling her a touching story about how we've learned so many valuable life-lessons today and how we don't want to go to jail."

"Perfect. That should keep her quiet," Eugene stated like an asshole.

"If you have any ideas, I'd love a better one."

"We bribe her with that Toblerone I saw in Gary's car."

"He's been through enough today without us stealing his Toblerone."

"It's in a hot car, Wes. Dogs die in hot cars. You know what else die in hot cars? Babies. That Toblerone was destined for barter lest it die a slow and melty death."

Eugene sounded particularly dumb because he was being particularly dumb. He didn't even think it was that funny of a thing to say. It was nothing, just an obnoxious waste of time. So why did he say it? Why did everything he said have to be a little joke, even when it wasn't funny? That's some shit he'd have to work through for the rest of his life.

"Enough, Gene," Wes said.

"Fine," Eugene said back with his voice. "But hey, I just thought of something."

"What?" Wes was intrigued. Did Eugene have an idea?

"How in the world is a school getting away with putting on an Andrew Lloyd Webber musical?"

"Great question, Gene. We should have fifteen-to-life to ponder the answer."

"Isn't it a little…" Eugene didn't want to use the word *rapey* and was trying to think of a different word. "Rapey?" he finally said. "For school, I mean?"

"Remember when we were in school and they let the drama club put on Frank Turner's adaptation of 'Birth of a Nation: The Musical'?" Wes asked while his brain tried its best to suppress more memories from said musical.

"Just because Frank Turner was president of the drama club. When he talked about adapting Birth of a Nation as a musical, I kind of thought he'd make the Ku Klux Klan less sympathetic than in the original film," Eugene reminisced. "But nope. If anything he made them straight up heroic!"

"I'm sure it was a hard task to make an adaptation of Birth of a Nation even more racist than the source material. But boy he did it! 'Good ol' Frank Turner,' they'd say. 'He did it,' they'd say. 'Good ol' super racist Frank Turner,' they'd say. The songs were catchy though."

"Oh the music was gorgeous," Eugene agreed. "If that's one thing I, or anyone, remembers about Frank Turner, it's that for being such a seething, unapologetic racist, he can write a damn catchy hook."

"I always felt bad about his club foot," Wes said before succeeding in suppressing more memories of that musical materializing in his mind's eye.

"Well it sounds like we've solved it, old friend." Eugene started pulling the coupon for an Arby's Jamocha Shake out from his pocket.

"We haven't solved anything yet and we certainly don't have time to go to Arby's. Put that coupon away. Do you recognize that car?"

Eugene did recognize that car, because it belonged to Lance McGrott, from work. Even more than the car, Eugene recognized Lance in the passenger seat and gross Joan in the driver's seat.

"I recognize that car and danger," he said to Wes.

"Why the fuck would they be here right now? Should we hide?" Wes asked.

"I thought you were done hiding, Iron Fist," Eugene said as they each hid behind a different car parked on the curb.

From behind their very secure and clever hiding spot, they watched Lance and Joan get out of the car. Joan walked around to the other side to help a still-injured Lance walk toward the school. If one looked closely, one might think that Joan was clutching Lance by the penis and butthole. The hole, not just his butt. And one would be right. She had several excuses as to why this was the best way for her to help Lance walk. In fact, it was a grand hindrance to the way he wanted to move, but she said he'd fall over without her help and he believed her. So her hands were on his penis and right in his butthole. But then they both stopped. Joan slowly turned her head in the direction of where Wes and Eugene were hiding. She seemed to be sniffing the air, like a bloodhound.

"Eugene?"

Joan said Eugene's name like she knew he was there. He didn't stand up.

"Yeah?" He said.

Wes looked at him with a face that wanted to say *shut the fuck up you gorilla* to him because that's basically what he wanted to say but not out loud.

"Are you here somewhere? I smell that stank on you." Wes kept looking at Eugene with the same face as described above.

"We are hiding behind this car," Eugene said.

Wes's face dropped, along with the rest of his head because of biological evolution.

"Oh," Joan said. "From us?"

"Yeah."

"Why?"

"Jesus Christ, Joan, I don't really know!" Eugene shouted.

He and Wes stood up, exposing themselves to the others. Specifically, their penises were hanging out. That wasn't mentioned before because it wasn't important. But now it makes sense and they put away their penises because it wasn't worth it for that one joke. Not everything said has to be a little joke. Their penises weren't even out. That part was made up. But the rest of everything was the absolute God's honest truth, written by the lord God himself because it was His plan.

Including this. And this. And even this part. It's all part of His plan.

"I knew I smelled your stank!" Joan said because of God's plan. Lance hadn't smelled any stank and was genuinely shocked to see Wes and Eugene standing there with their penises out.

"Wesley," Lance said. Wes prepared himself for the worst. "I… am sorry."

Wes did not expect that sentence to end the way it did.

"You're sorry he kicked your stupid ass! Remember?" Eugene talked a lot. "He was all '*Ka-boooorm into the big cooker's bellyyyy*' and you were all 'Ahhh my face hurts because *I'm a dumb dick!*'"

"Wes, I am sorry for the years of misery I put you through," Lance said, ignoring Eugene's accurate summery of earlier events. "I had no right treating you the way I did. It shouldn't have taken physical action for me to realize that and I hope it never comes to blows like that again. I'm truly, truly sorry."

"See what one savage beating did?" Wes said to Eugene. He turned back to Lance and Joan. "So, what are you two doing at this school, anyway?"

"I was going to try out for a musical they're putting on," Lance said.

"I drove him here because a big strong man beat him off too much for him to drive by himself," Joan said.

"Down," Wes corrected. "A big strong man beat him down. And you know that it's a musical for children to perform, right? High school kids."

"Not this year," Lance said. "They're going community theater style and opening it to the public. Anybody can audition if they want."

Wes and Eugene looked at each other and gave a nod in the realization that there were no holes in this plot. It all made perfect sense. It was God's plan, after all.

"Isn't that why you're here?" Lance asked. "To audition?"

"Yes." Wes said convincingly.

While they stood chatting, a couple dozen or so people went in and out of the school. Making the high-school production of Phantom of the Opera open to the community certainly made it a popular place during the auditions. Among the throngs of people seemingly everywhere, Eugene spotted a boy he recognized with a grown-up lady. He recognized this boy because of God's plan and because he'd beaten him into a bloody mess either yesterday or the day before. It was Jake Mortinburg and his mom! Eugene does a lot of things without thinking, including blurting out a greeting to a child he recognized.

"Hey Jake," Eugene casually said.

Wes turned and saw what was happening and wasn't the least bit happy about it. Jake and his mom turned around in surprise as well. Eugene covered by continuing.

"Uh... good luck auditioning!"

"I'm not auditioning! Plays are gay! My cousin is auditioning!"

Jake's mom didn't seem to care that he used the word *gay* the way he did. Eugene suspected she might be part of the problem. She then leaned down and spoke to her son.

"Jake, who's that man? Do you know him?"

Jake eyed Eugene up and down slowly and suspensefully. No one liked how long it was taking him to answer. Fuck.

"Just some douche bag, I don't know!" he finally said.

"How does he know you?" his mom asked.

"Probably because of my awesome viral videos, Mom!"

This seemed to be an acceptable answer. Or it was a terrible answer. Either way, she wanted to leave, so Jake and his mom entered the school.

"I wonder who else is here," Eugene said.

"Well it was great catching up guys, I really felt like we grew a lot as people just now." Wes was trying to ditch the others. "But we have to get on with it."

Joan took that opportunity to grab Lance again by the penis and butthole and "help" him into the school after saying some awkward goodbyes. Once they were inside the building, Wes and Eugene started to make their way to the playground around back.

That was also the time six police cars pulled up to the front of the school. Wes and Eugene figuratively froze by literally standing still. Red and blue lights were illuminating everything around like some sort of patriotic disco. Before Wes and Eugene could even start to think about what to do next, a door opened on the first police car in the line and a police officer got out.

"This is the police!" said a loud voice through a megaphone.

"I don't know if they need to announce that," Eugene quietly said to Wes. "Seems redundant." Although he agreed, Wes was mostly relieved that the voice wasn't Evan's as it continued.

"This school is now a restricted area. You are to evacuate the property immediately and stand clear of the body. I repeat, this property is now a crime scene and is to be evacuated."

236

It seemed like everyone in town was here, and they all started to flee the scene at once. Parents, teachers, children, and other volunteers and employees flooded out of the building like some sort of other flood-like analogy. Wes and Eugene continued to stand figuratively frozen and the scene unfolded around them.

If this was a movie, it would probably be one of those cool shots where the focus of the frame, Wes and Eugene, stay relatively static while everything else is sped up to give the feeling of isolating urgency as the camera slowly pans wide. And there would probably be some sort of mid 2000s indie-rock song playing that features lots of reverby-guitars and a heavy electronic beat. Depending on the director. *A box office hit*, they'd say! Wes played back what the police man just said in his mind instead of imagining what this would look like as a movie.

"Did he just say 'the body'?" Wes asked Eugene.

Eugene was imagining what was playing out in front of them as a zany, mad-cap romp-type movie with *Yakkity Sax* playing as people ran away with sound effects like *boings* and that sound Fred Flintstone's feet make when he runs, which is probably someone playing rapid sixteenth-notes on two different-sized wood blocks.

"What?" Eugene said.

"I think that cop just said 'the body' like maybe there's a body somewhere here that used to be alive but isn't anymore!"

"What?" Eugene used that same word, but this time he meant its use to be that of surprise, not that he again didn't hear what Wes said. Wes picked that up but was still annoyed about it. He started to move against the current of the people leaving and Eugene followed.

They thrust themselves thoroughly through the thick throng, though they thought that they thumped three therapists through the thirteen thick, thorny thistles.

"Fuck," Wes managed to say once the two were within eyeshot of the horrible scene. The pit Wes had felt in his stomach over the word *body* was justified.

"Oh shit, I totally called it!" Eugene said as he saw Ms. Caldwell lying dead on the cold concrete of the playground.

He reached for a high-five from Wes, but was left hanging. He awkwardly lowered his hand when he realized he was intentionally being dissed.

"Gene, we are responsible for a death," Wes said, almost not believing what he was saying.

By now there were ten police officers and various other people with badges and licenses and rubber gloves and bags and blankets all around the gross corpse.

"This is something we're going to have to deal with forever. It's going to weigh on your consciences until we're also gone."

It was hitting him hard and leaving him in shock. The sound of the officials' chattering started to enter his ears.

"So what did she die of, anyway? Is there any analysis or hypothesis yet?" One officer said to another.

"Well, judging by the track marks on her arm, she was a junkie," the other officer said.

"So she OD'd?"

"Yeah, I'm thinking. Look at the yellow foam around her mouth. Classic sign."

"She's also got a huge roll of cash in her pocket. Between that and the contraband, I'd say without a doubt that she was pushing drugs on the children at this school."

"What a horrible, horrible woman. I'm glad she's dead."

"Me too. You know, I'm not even going to investigate any further to see if there was any other foul play."

"Me neither. Spread the word around. Let's get this cleaned up so we can get to Arby's before they close."

The conversation the two protagonists just overheard was making Eugene feel very smug.

"What were you saying, Wes?" He asked, smugly.

"Wow," Wes said now in a different sort of shock. "Shooting up junk on a school playground. In front of kids. Just to be a bitch. God dammit she one-hundred percent sucked! God dammit! Fuck it, I'm done."

"Yep," Eugene agreed. "Looks like we have nothing to worry about after all. So if you've got nothing else going on…"

"Eugene, would you like to join me for an Arby's roast beef sandwich and a Jamocha Shake?" Wes asked his very excited friend.

Unfortunately, Eugene's flailing, spastic motion at finally getting to go to Arby's caught the attention of four eyeballs belonging to two men who were currently hiding across the playground behind some bushes. Those two men were not thinking Arby's. In fact, they weren't hungry for food at all. Thirsty, yes: blood-thirsty. For blood. The blood of Wes and Eugene. Because it was Evan and Wade who owned those four eyeballs. Two in each of their faces.

"Detective," Evan said to Wade while his face turned red under his ski-mask. "It's those two fuckfaces who tasered us!"

"Today is the day we charge them for their sins," Wade said like a friggin' psychopath.

"I'm going in. I'm shooting to kill." Evan meant it.

"No." Wade put his pinky-finger into the barrel of Evan's gun. "It's not time yet. Patience is the key ingredient of this delicious murder-pie."

With that strange statement, a commotion arose. Almost out of nowhere, everyone who had moments ago been ordered to evacuate the premises came flooding back behind the school. People were getting shoved around while the police tried to keep the growing crowd away from the crime scene. Whistles were blown and palms of hands held high. Sticks were swung around as order was trying to be maintained. The entire playground was now packed wall-to-wall and shoulder-to-shoulder with a large percentage of the community. Evan's visuals on Wes and Eugene were obstructed, to say the least. The police megaphone came back out.

"*This is the police!*" the amplified voice said.

"You're right, that's pretty unnecessary," Wes said to Eugene.

"*We need everyone to evacuate the property! What are all of you still doing here?*" The police officer sounded desperate. Everyone started talking at once.

"*QUIET! Please, one at a time!*" Among those who bolted toward the scene was Henry. He was in a right panic and answered the police's question.

"There's a big bee hive out front and a bunch of bees are coming out of it!"

"Hey, it's that kid," Eugene said.

"I like that kid," Wes affirmed.

"Wait, he doesn't go to this school. Why is he here?"

"I think we're past that, Gene. Everyone in town is here to audition for the play. It checks out," Wes said.

"What play?" Eugene asked.

"*Little boy*," the police man said to Henry through the megaphone, "*Did you say there are a bunch of bees out front?*"

"A whole hive!" he answered.

"Exactly one hivesworth," said the English cab driver. "I'd say it's two stone, innit? One hivesworth?"

"*And*," the police man, still speaking through his megaphone, was trying to make sense of this. "*You are all allergic to bees?*" Everyone in the crowd nodded politely, remembering the officer's request to not all speak at once.

"*Okay, well, we certainly don't want anyone to get stung. Just please stay out of our way. We have to do something about this terrible woman who died over here. She smells like piss and it's gross. So stay a little back, okay?*" Everyone nodded again and politely back away about a foot, except the English cab driver, who backed up about 30 centimeters.

"Hey, since you're all here, I might as well ask." The police officer seemed to have something else on his mind as he spoke through the megaphone. *"Have any of you here run across a couple of guys in ski masks?"*

"Ski masks!" Eugene said to Wes. "That's what they're called!"

"You've probably seen on the news, but a couple of losers in masks and hats keep terrorizing kids. Anybody have any leads? See anything suspicious?"

"You mean like those ghosts in the bushes?" Henry said.

Everyone figuratively froze. Their heads turned in unison toward the bushes. Even and Wade dramatically stood up. Everyone was surprised, but none more than Wes and Eugene, who had a weird couple of days.

"Is that what we looked like?" Eugene asked Wes quietly.

"Must be," Wes said back. "So. Who in the holy tap-dancing fuck do you think they are?"

"Do you supposed," as Eugene started to speak he already kind of knew the answer to the question he was about to ask. "Do you suppose we are going to invent time-travel after all and that's-" Wes cut him off.

"No."

"Yeah, I just…" Eugene never finished that sentence. But even if he had tried, he would have been interrupted by the word *freeze* being shouted and a baker's dozen guns being lifted and pointed in the direction of the bushes.

"*You two!*" the police officer shouted through his megaphone. "*Hands where I can see them!*" Wade raised his hands and calmly spoke.

"It's okay officer. We are under cover."

Wade nudged Evan and they both lifted their masks. Wes and Eugene were now very thoroughly confused and scared.

"You see," Wade started, but he would never finish that sentence. He was interrupted by the shout of a child. Two words.

"*Snake bite!*"

Jake Mortinburg and a dozen-or-so other children emerged from the crowd and rushed toward the bushes. Jake jumped on Wade's chest and knocked him to the ground. He took his thumb and jammed it into Wade's nostril. His index finger met his thumb through the nostril skin and Jake started just fucking tearing at Wade's nose from the inside. There was immediate blood. Jake's other hand had become a fist and was forcing itself down onto Wade's skull over and over again. Wade did not have a plan for what was happening.

At the same time, two boys jumped onto Evan and took him down next to wade. One kid held Evan's eyes open while another spit and smeared boogers onto the unprotected eyeballs. Yet another child was doing seat-drops onto Evan's ribcage, knocking the wind out of his lungs. Even was also very confused and terrified. He used his strength to turn to wade, who was trying to pull a kid's hand out of his nose. They made eye contact and silently communicated that they needed to fight back.

Evan rolled and managed to pin three kids under his body while he reared his hands and started to open-palm slap all three across the face. Wade tore the fingers from his nostril and bent the boy's index finger back until the bone snapped. There was a scream followed by uncontrollable tears and snot coming out of the kid's face.

By this point, no one knew what in the serious flying fuck was happening.

"*What?!*" An officer yelled. "What the *hell* is happening?!"

"Those ghosts are scaring Jake Mortinburg pretty bad!" Henry told the cop, adding to his confusion. Wes saw an opportunity.

"Boy officer. I don't know, but I heard about these two dudes who were beating up kids on playgrounds." Eugene picked up on what Wes was doing and contributed.

"It sure looks like you've caught those monsters red-handed. Do they match any descriptions you may or may not have?"

The officer thought long and hard. As a matter of fact, the description he was remembering was the very same as what he was seeing currently with his own eyes!

"Now that I think about it," the policeman said, "those two guys are bad news. Unstable. I've been watching them off and on for the past month and I thought it was stemming from them having a secret, self-hating love affair. But child-beating psychos also checks out."

"Look, Officer," Wes put on his serious voice, "I would never tell you how to do your job. But I would ask if you planned on doing anything about what's going on."

"Didn't I see that those guys tasered a kid?" Eugene asked nonchalantly. "They might still have it somewhere and I'm sure it's covered in their finger prints and not anyone else's." No one reacted to what he said. "They also like abusing hookers."

"Good enough for me!" The police officer directed his megaphone toward Evan and Wade.

"*This is the police!*" Wes and Eugene rolled their eyes. "*Officer Thomas and Detective Wadeler! Remove yourselves from the scene and come with me. Now!*"

"Bullshit, Officer Suck!" Evan wasn't having it. "You back the fuck off!"

He quickly drew his gun and fired it once in the air. Everything around him stopped as he kept talking.

"I'm going to shoot those two idiots you're standing near. And then I'm shooting every one of those little shits who were punching me and stuff!"

The air was stiff and still. Nobody had quite processed the horror that came out of Evan's mouth. He'd been talking shit his whole life, but this was different. It wasn't funny. Nothing was funny. He just threatened to murder thirteen children. Who knows if he'd continue and take everyone else out as well. What about Wade? Was he on board for this? It got real. The weight of that sentence hit Wes full-force.

"Evan, your fight is with me."

Wes was trying to come across as calm and in control. But he wasn't. He was terrified. Not of his own death, but what else could happen in these next few moments.

"No one else has to get shot today."

Evan lifted his pistol until it was aimed right at Wes's nose.

"Maybe Eugene, too," Wed added, "but seriously no one else."

Eugene made that sound that people make sometimes that's like a *tss* and goes with a head bob. It tends to communicate a sort of sarcastic *typical*. Wade picked up a fouth-grade kid next to him and tossed him about seven feet to the side. It was rude. The kid had a bruised elbow from it, but nothing serious. Wes was alarmed.

"Take it out on me, Evan! Shoot me if you're going to, but let the children go! Full disclosure, I'd prefer if you didn't shoot me. Just so we're clear. But regardless, let everyone else out of here."

"It's a good start." Evan's finger twitched on the trigger. He took one step closer to Wes. "Goodbye, you piss-drinking, butt-fucking shit-stain! Say hi to the devil from me."

Wes shut his eyes. This was it. At least he told Bonnie how he felt. If he was dying in a second, that would be what he'd think about as it happened. If this was a movie, there'd be a cool montage of what could have been with Bonnie and Wes's future history playing over some ambient jazz but with random reversed sound effects so the audience would know it isn't reality. *Box office hit!* Wes stood with his eyes closed.

Because Wes's eyes were closed, he didn't see that Jake Mortinburg, who was *not* there to audition for the play but to watch his cousin audition, was slithering across the grass on his stomach. In fact, everyone's eyes were locked on Evan's gun so no one else around saw Jake Mortinburg slithering across the grass on his stomach. Well, some of the children saw him but didn't make a scene because of it. There was a gun out. There was a knife out. Jake Mortinburg had a pocket knife in his teeth.

When he was within arm's reach of the stand-off, he reached out and sliced Evan's Achilles tendon! Evan let out a very loud and embarrassing scream. He immediately fell backward but the surprise motivated his already itchy trigger-finger to contract.

BANG!

As Evan fell and his gun shot a bullet, his aim was compromised because of gravity. The bullet raced through the air directly at Eugene. He absently sensed it play out. As an act of survival, his mind slowed reality down enough for him to perceive an impending bullet about to end his existence, but not to have any ideas for stopping his own murder. In a twinkling, he accepted his fate and he braced for impact. This all happened very fast. He almost didn't notice Joan's voice because of what his brain was going through. But her voice was loud and determined.

"*No! Noooooooo! No! No! Noooooo no no!*" She shouted as she was shot.

She had also noticed Eugene being in the crossfire and acted fast. She knew the risk, but she also didn't want to be in a world that didn't have a Eugene in it. Also, while she was jumping in front of him, her nipple came out. Nobody would figure it out until later, but she intentionally took her nipple out on purpose. She collapsed onto the ground similarly to how it would be if someone threw a sealed plastic bag full of ABC gum against any surfaced and studied the results. Results are in: not great.

"*Joan!*" Eugene finally said. "*Fuck! What?!* You saved me!" Now who was being redundant?

With Evan on the ground and Wade looking stunned about what the crap was going on, the police officers started shooting.

One, two, three, four. Four kneecaps. That's how many kneecaps were shot just then; two belonging to Evan and two belonging to Wade. Now they were both on the ground screaming like little babies. Dumb little stupid babies.

"Hey Evan," Wes said to Evan. His eyes moved to meet Wes's. "I'd rather eat a piss sandwich and still have two wonderfully-functioning legs than to have just been shot in the kneecaps. So fuck you, brother! I win! Even without time-travel!" Evan didn't get Wes's point about time travel so he continued to cry like a bitch.

One, two, three, four. Four police officers then carried the men away like they were team lifting a couple of couches. But they weren't couches. They were two men with severely damaged knee caps. As the men were carried away, Eugene reached out and honked Wade's nose before turning his attention to the victim.

Eugene leaned over Joan. He looked right at her nipple. He didn't look away. It wasn't the best nipple he'd ever seen, far from it! But it was a nipple and he looked at it. There were worse things to look at than a nipple. Anyone's. He felt... sad? Probably sad, or close to it. He was worried. He didn't want to be looking at a dead lady's nipple. He leaned in and spoke softly.

"Joan?"

He was still looking at her nipple. It was the perfect scenario because it seemed like he was trying to see if she was breathing. But nope.

"Joan, are you alive?"

Everyone around was looking. They were also all backing away inch by inch. Wes wasn't looking. His eyes were shut. He didn't like what was happening because it was all terrible. He almost just died! Joan's nipple moved. That was followed by a cough. Blood came out of her mouth. Her eyes didn't open.

"Eugene?"

"Yeah Joan, I'm right here."

"Can you come closer?"

Eugene got on his knees and leaned his face close to hers.

"What? What can I do?" he asked without knowing if he meant what he was asking.

Joan then took a deep breath through her nose. It seemed like she was struggling to breathe. Another deep breath through her nose. And another.

"Joan, are you smelling me?" Eugene knew the answer to his question.

"You…" she was having a little trouble speaking.

"got that…"

"What, Joan?" He asked tenderly.

"Stank." She finished her sentence.

"I do got that stank, Joan!" Wes opened his eyes. He wasn't sure what to believe anymore.

"Eugene, I love how much you care about kids. The fact that you and Wes were out trying to bring in those playground terrorists, and then were willing to get shot in their defense. It's enough to…"

Joan didn't finish her sentence. She couldn't. Her mouth was suddenly plugged up with Eugene's tongue. He grabbed her jowls and kissed like he really meant it! She lost herself in the moment, and fainted. Possibly from the blood-loss but also because of the pure euphoria she'd just reached from the unsolicited kiss. Eugene pulled back. He locked eyes with Wes, who was in shock for several different reasons by now. He looked around the crowd and everyone was looking back at him. Jake Mortinburg was still on his stomach holding a bloody knife. No one was moving. Eugene addressed them all with his public-speaking voice.

"Hey, does anyone know if there are still a bunch of bees out front? I'm supposed to be somewhere."

CHAPTER 12: Fucking Finally

Everything smelled like hot oil and meat. The table wasn't particularly clean. There were grease spots and salt everywhere. There were piles upon piles of little wadded-up balls of foil. Emptied sauce-packets found their way to the floor with no one else there to care enough to take any note of their escape. Nearby paper cups featured dairy dripping down their sides into little muddy pools on the tabletop.

"Another round?" Eugene asked.

"What a dumb question. Go!" Wes was right.

Of course all four of them wanted yet another roast-beef sandwich! Because this was Arby's, goddammit! Eugene got up from his seat next to Joan and went back to the counter for a third time. Wes hurried to finish his sandwich so he'd be ready for the next.

"And get potato cakes!" he added. Eugene turned around.

"You don't want more curly fries? Those are almost gone." Eugene was legitimately concerned.

"Both," Wes answered through a mouthful of half-chewed beef and bread. Eugene nodded.

Bonnie moved closer against Wes on their bench. She was still working on her second roast-beef sandwich and had some serious catching up to do. She was also the only one at the table at all concerned with how much Joan was bleeding through her clothes.

"Joan," Bonnie started.

Joan's eyes snapped up to Bonnie's the way a werewolf eating a dog might react to being caught. It startled Bonnie and she made a weird sound and some of her food came out of her mouth.

"*Glert!*"

Joan was taken aback by the glert and thought she should spit out a piece of her food at Bonnie. Instead she repeated the weird sound with a full mouth, and that *glert* left her mouth along with a bit of chewed food on its own without her even trying. Bonnie decided not to say anything and went back to eating her sandwich. Instead, she'd just try to keep her meal away from the blood Joan was dripping everywhere.

"Joan, will you keep your blood away from our feast please?" Wes asked. Bonnie was relieved that Wes was on the same page as her.

"I know you didn't want to go to the hospital and I respect that. I disagree with your choice with every fiber of my being, but I respect your right to choose what to do with your body because I'm not a monster. But do something about that."

Wes pointed to her wound. It seemed like it was exactly where the human heart should be, but Joan didn't seem that phased by it.

"I got the bullet out, buttface." She called Wes a buttface. "I threw it in the trash and stuffed the blood-hole with Arby's napkins. It's fine!"

The length some people go through when they're thinkin' Arby's. Nobody was satisfied with Joan's explanation of her self first-aid care but more than that they were still hungry for delicious roast-beef. Luckily, Eugene reappeared with a whole new tray of individually-wrapped roast-beef sandwiches, and curly fries and potato cakes.

"The trick is that even though you know you're going to eat maybe a half-dozen of them, don't get them all at once. Get them fresh as you go. They'll be hot every time and you're not limited by a predetermined number you'll soon regret."

He placed a sandwich from the tray in front of each other person at the table while narrating.

"A Arby's sandwich for you, a Arby's sandwich for you, a Arby's sandwich for you, and a Arby's sandwich for me!"

Suddenly the other three weren't as hungry. The feeling of momentary discomfort passed and they dug in.

"You know what I love?" Eugene asked. "Arby's." He took a giant bite of his roast-beef sandwich.

"I'm glad you guys still have appetites after everything that happened to you," Bonnie said.

"What do you mean?" Eugene asked with a too-full mouth.

"What do I mean?" Bonnie asked. "Well, you know…" She picked up a curly fry. "Getting playground justice for elementary school students and getting two crooked law enforcement officers sent to jail. It seems like maybe you learned a lot."

She ate the fry without knowing it was the one Eugene wanted. It was the small-curl kind that is most likely from the center of the bigger curls, but it was two and three-quarter inches long. When Eugene was a boy, he used to hold that type of curly fry up to each side of his face where sideburns belong and say he was a Hasidic Jew. He doesn't really do that anymore because someone told him once it was racist. He didn't understand why and still knows in his heart that it's a sold bit of comedy but some types of humor just don't age well.

"What did we learn?" Wes repeated.

"I learned that Wes can throw a punch!" Eugene said. "Remember when that guy at work was all 'Ahh You're punching me and I can't take it because I'm not a man' and you were all 'But I *am* a man and that's precisely why I'm punching you so hard' Hwoo*pah smash!*" Wes was slightly annoyed that Eugene was still on this kick of re-telling that story. He decided to indulge his friend regardless, just this once.

"Yeah, that was pretty sweet. And you were all 'Oh *holy shit Wes you're awesome!*" Wes and Eugene giggled as they each took another bite of delicious food.

"Did I ever tell you guys about the one night I got Arby's and it was weird, wet beef?" Eugene asked. No one reacted. "Did I? Wes, did I tell you that?"

"Isn't beef," Wes slowly started to say, "supposed to be wet? Like, it's not supposed to be dry…"

"Not like that. At all!" Eugene was simultaneously reliving how strange this happenstance was for him and getting excited to tell them all about it.

"I was driving home from seeing a concert an hour from town and of course I wanted Arby's. I knew there was one up ahead so I got a large roast-beef sandwich, curly fries and mozzarella sticks." Joan was already lost in his story. "As I sunk my teeth into the sandwich, I thought something was different. Not bad, but different. I went for another bite and concluded that what was making this different was that the beef was wet. But not moist."

Joan loved that he said *moist*. She loved that word.

"I took another bite because I didn't know if I liked this or not. It was like they took the pile of beef and dunked it through their Au Jus sauce before slapping it into the toasted bun, which, by the way was getting soggier and losing structural integrity with every passing moment. After another bite, the sandwich was half-gone and I was done. It was dripping all down my arm and onto my pants and seat. I was getting this sandwich juice all over the steering wheel and everything! So I wadded it all back into the wrapper and threw it in my litter bag, conceding that I would just eat the fries and mozzarella sticks, which were delicious."

"That's a huge drag you didn't get to eat your whole sandwich though," Wes empathized.

"But here's the awesome part," Eugene said. "So this whole process ended up taking me about twenty minutes. By then I was in another little town and coming up on…" he paused for drama, "*Another* Arby's! So I got a whole new sandwich! And, I also got another order of curly fries and mozzarella sticks!" Wes and Joan both looked enthusiastic as he finished his story.

"Plus, since it was the same order as the one from twenty minutes ago, I remembered the exact amount I was getting charged and said it at the same time the guy at the drive-through did." No one knew why Eugene was excited about that part. "That sandwich was spot-on. Perfect."

"Did you tell the dude about the wet sandwich from the next town over?" Joan asked.

"Nope!" Eugene said and took a giant bite.

Although she enjoyed the story, Bonnie wasn't ready to drop addressing the issues at hand. Joan also enjoyed the story. She took one hand off of her roast-beef sandwich and put it on Eugene's lap. He stopped chewing. Her hand crept up his thigh.

"I love roast-beef and I love hand jobs," Eugene said to Wes and Bonnie's surprised.

Without the context of the impending old-fashioned undertable, it seemed like a pretty strange thing to say.

"But one distracts from the other. When I'm done with my feast of shaved-meat, you may proceed to pull on my beef-boner."

"Glert." Bonnie made a sound out of surprise and a bit of food fell from her mouth onto the table.

"Why do you keep saying that?" Joan asked.

"What?" Bonnie said. They looked at each other. Then Joan processed what Eugene had just said.

"Hold on. I can manhandle your man stick once you're done eating?" Joan was pleased. "And you'll smack around my fat tits?"

"Why not," Eugene said and he drank the remaining curly fries out of one of the containers. The ratio of fries to salt, pepper, and crumbs wasn't ideal, though Eugene gave not but a single fuck regarding the matter.

"No, but really," Bonnie said. "You two didn't learn a single thing over the last couple of days? Didn't you lose your jobs for beating up your boss? You saw how those little fifth-grade shits started beating up Evan and Wade, so they are obviously still little terrors and will probably to continue to fuck with other children. What about your cars? Gary's in the hospital! Oh, I should bring him an Arby's sandwich when we're done here. And one for Jeremy, too. And maybe the sitter. But for what I'm paying her she can buy her own damn Arby's!"

"Oh my god, somebody's a real miss fucking chatterbox tonight!" Eugene said, rudely.

"Shut up, Gene," Wes said. "Bonnie, what are you talking about? I learned how to use a taser. Is that what you mean?"

"I can't believe you guys!" Bonnie was getting worked up. "Don't you realize how lucky you are? You narrowly avoided life in prison! You just blamed somebody else for the awful things you were doing!"

"Right, but those gaycist cops deserved it," Wes told her.

"But you two *also* deserved it!" You were guilty!" she told his guilty ass.

"Gene, where did you get tasers, anyway? I looked it up and there's no taser store," Wes said. Eugene sighed.

"I got 'em off Gregslist, okay?" Eugene answered rudely with a mouthful of Arby's.

"Craigslist?" Wes asked.

"Craigslist?" Eugene also asked. "Who's Craig?"

"Who's Greg?!" Wes demanded.

"Greg from Gregslist! He lives like ten minutes from town. He's got a website full of stuff he has in his garage."

"So you bought them from a dude named Greg?" Wes asked.

"No, you don't *buy* it," Eugene said. "You challenge him and if you win you can pick out something he has in his garage."

"Wait, you fought a dude named Greg for some tasers?" Bonnie asked while Joan got excited.

"No I didn't *fight* him. I challenged him to a singing contest and I won because he has a terrible falsetto. I won two contests in a row so I got his two tasers."

"Who judges the contests?" The answers Wes was getting out of Eugene were only leading to more questions.

"We both do. It's usually pretty obvious who the winners are. It's all on the honor system." Eugene was becoming more and more indignant. "Look, he's not out to scam anybody if that's what you're asking! It's all very fair. Check out his website, dude. He's legit! Gregslist slash com."

"Slash com? Not 'dot'?" For some reason this was the most surprising thing to Wes about the whole shebang. "Why on earth does he do this?" asked Wes.

"What am I, his biographer? I don't know, dude! Who's your best buddy Craig I'm hearing all about all of a sudden?"

"Craigslist." Wes said thinking that would explain things. It didn't. Eugene looked at him in a way that implied anticipating more information.

"Look, I don't know anything more about Craig."

"Well at least I've met Greg," said Eugene. Check-mate.

"Guys, the more I think about this and learn about Gregs and Craigs," Bonnie said with a quiver, "I just don't know what else I can take. You must have gleaned some sort of life-altering meaning from everything that's happened. The fact that you seem to not have done that is alarming to me!"

"Wes, she's ruining my beef-buzz," Eugene glerted through food.

"Your what?" Bonnie asked.

"Beef buzz," Wes repeated. "It's when you feel drunk off of beef because you've eaten so much of it. Like all warm and full but tired and slaphappy."

Eugene nodded as he picked up his half-full Jamocha Shake and loudly sucked the rest of it through the little plastic straw. With all of the talk, no one noticed that Joan had two of her fingers stuck inside her roast-beef sandwich. With her other hand, she had two fingers in her vaginal canal.

"Bonnie, you're saying a lot of crazy things right now that I know you don't mean," Wes said as the word *crazy* suddenly triggered a memory. "Crazy like ol' Frank Turner's adaptation of the musical Jefferson School is about to put on. Remember, Gene?"

"Oh Shit! 'Frank Turner's Andrew Lloyd Webber's Phantom of the Opera!' I forgot all about that!" Eugene was excited and put off all at once.

"I still can't believe that he just replaced the hideous monster in a mask with 'a Mexican.' His words, not mine," Wes added for clarity.

"Ol' racist Frank Turner," Eugene remembered. "But the music was stunning!"

"Gorgeous!" Wes agreed. "Bonnie, you're saying a lot of non-racist-yet-still-crazy things right now. But that doesn't change how I feel about you."

He noticed Joan smelling both of her hands at the same time and didn't ask why. He thought he might know and he was right but it was never addressed. Bonnie wasn't sure she liked where this conversation was headed. She was pretty exhausted from the events of God's plan.

"Wes, I know we have a lot to talk about. But maybe now isn't the time. Let's just finish our food and go home."

"There is no finish!" Eugene said as he ate half of a potato cake.

"Bonnie, no. I've put this off for too long as it is." Wes was getting real.

"Put what off, Wes?" Bonnie was getting nervous.

"Put off, ignored, repressed, all of the above." Wes stood up out of his seat. "Bonnie, you know I've always been crazy about you. You were my best friend my whole life and you always will be." Those words stung Eugene right in the gizzards.

"Hey! Fuck you!" Eugene said as he threw a half of potato cake at Wes and missed.

"Bonnie, you are my best friend in a very different way than how Eugene is also my best friend." Wes looked at Eugene for approval and got it. He continued. "It's been a weird couple of days. We've never ever really had a fight before. In our whole lives we've never had a real fight until now. The one thing that really shook me up in this whole mess was the thought of losing you. I can't imagine a world where I can't call you whenever I want to tell you I heard Rob Paulson doing another voice on a cartoon." Wes's voice started to crack slightly. "And I know you don't really care but you seem happy that I'm excited to hear a voice actor I like in so many different cartoons. I love watching those cartoons with you and Jeremy and I love playing with him and I love that you stay up with me and have a beer or two after he goes to bed." Wes's eyes were welling up.

"Wes, look." Bonnie sounded exhausted. "I'm not mad. Well, I'm not happy about this, but we can work it out another time. There will be a better time for this."

"All of the time," Wes said as he got down on one knee. "I want to be with you all of the time."

"Oh shit!" Bonnie glerted.

Eugene stopped chewing. Joan stopped smelling her hands. Then she started smelling her hands again. Wes reached to the table and grabbed the most , round, the most golden, the most perfect curly fry piece that there ever was. He held it proudly toward her.

"Bonnie, will you be my wife? And make irreverent observations with Eugene and me for all of time?" Eugene was happy to be a part of this proposal.

"Wes," Eugene butted in. "Much like the uncircumcised Rabbi, this is highly unorthodox!"

Eugene had still been thinking about his Hasidic Jew joke from before and determined that even if this joke was culturally insensitive, it was still a solid bit of business and he was sticking to his guns. Unfortunately, it was not a great time for jokes. Even if one has a strong, solid bit of business, one must still read the room and determine if the timing and context are appropriate.

"I don't want to ever worry about losing you again." Wes was serious.

Bonnie said nothing. There was a lot going through her mind, including the notion that she was over-thinking. It was an excruciating silence.

Bonnie's hand slowly inched toward Wes's. Wes watched her hand. Her small, soft, beautiful hand. Her digits approached the curly fry and she slipped the orange, greasy junk-food around her ring finger and looked at it like it was a solid-gold, diamond encrusted curly fry. What on Earth could be better than that?

"Yes!" She said. "*Yes Wes yes Wes* I will marry you!"

Everyone in the booth lit up. Bonnie stood up out of the seat and embraced her new fiancé. They kissed. Then hugged. Then kissed again. Wes grabbed her butt. She liked it. She grabbed his butt. He liked it. They were into that. Joan watched them both have each other's hands on their butts. She liked it. Eugene swallowed the last bite of his final sandwich. He liked it. Joan noticed that Eugene was done eating. She stood up out of the booth.

"Eugene, you know I've always been crazy about you," Joan said as she reached for a curly fry and started to bend to one knee. "This half hour or so," she continued before getting interrupted.

"I'm not marrying you, Joan." Eugene said.

"Fair enough," she said as she got back into the booth." How about that hand job, then?"

"How about that hand-job, Joan?" Eugene said like a man who was about to get a hand job in his favorite restaurant after eating his favorite meal of several Arby's roast beef sandwiches, various sides and two Jamocha Shakes.

They all laughed together as Joan unzipped his pants. It was at that moment the door to Arby's swung open loudly and a lady stomped in like she owned the place. Eugene noticed out of the corner of his eye that she looked just like Daria, from Daria. He turned to confirm his suspicion and then turned to see if Wes noticed, whose hand was still on Bonnie's awesome butt.

"*Holy shit*, don't start hand-jobbing me yet, Joan!"

Eugene said this too loud. The young lady turned and spotted the group at the table. Eugene waved. She waved back without smiling, and then approached the group.

"Why are you bleeding so much?" the slut from the thrift store asked Joan.

"Got shot," she replied. "It's whatever though."

"Rad," the slut said.

"What are you doing here?" Eugene asked excitedly.

"You said you were coming here later," she replied emotionless. "I figured right now you were either here at Arby's or dead and I was curious which it was. Plus, I have this coupon for a Jamocha Shake."

She held a coupon out for Eugene to see. He grabbed her hand and pulled it right up to his eye and stared suspiciously at it.

"Where did you get this?!" he asked the way one might ask that same question to a person holding an unlabeled jar of milk.

"In the mail, stupid. They send Arby's coupons in the mail like every day."

"Right," Eugene said. "Well I'm glad you said something about it because I forgot to use mine."

"You fucking idiot," Wes said, "that's all you've talked about for days."

"Everyone stop calling me dumb, for fuck's sake! I'll use it on my next one!" Eugene replied.

"How many are you going to have?" the girl from the Thrift store asked, noticing at least three empty Arby's cups dripping with Jamocha.

"As many as I want," Eugene told her. "I don't really concern myself too much with committing to numbers. Hey speaking of which, Joan was about to give me a greasy, seasoned curly fry-flavored hand job under the table."

"That's cool I guess," she said. "Can I watch or like play with your balls or something?"

"I'm into it," Joan said very seriously.

"I don't care if you get blood on me," she said to Joan.

Eugene was stunned. He looked over at Wes. Wes nodded. He looked at Bonnie. She nodded. Eugene looked at Joan. She licked her lips. He looked at that slut he barely knew. She shrugged and walked across the table to get to the other side of Eugene and squeezed into the space next to him.

One, two, three, four. Four hands. That's how many hands dropped below the table and onto Eugene's lap. Eugene smiled and grabbed what was left of his third Jamocha shake. He sucked the rest of it down lazily while he was jerked-off and fondled to completion right there in the Arby's booth. Eugene was starting to think that this was the best Christmas Day ever! It was Christmas, after all.

"What a weird couple of days!" he said.

THE END

Thank you for reading my book! You win a prize! Below is a link to a FREE COPY of my album *Automaton*. Feel free to check out more of my original music on Amazon, iTunes, Spotify, and many other music platforms. -Dan

Automaton free download:
tinyurl.com/n4wtfkv

Find Dan Louisell on the internet:

dan.louisell@gmail.com
facebook.com/dan.louisell
twitter: @DanLouisell

CPSIA information can be obtained
at www.ICGtesting.com
Printed in the USA
BVOW08s0239181217
503092BV00002B/625/P

9 781979 746519